1997

Top 10 Technologies

and Their Impact on CPAs

Sandi Smith, CPA, CMA, CDP

AMERICAN INSTITUTE OF CERTIFIED PUBLIC ACCOUNTANTS

AICPA Technology Series

NOTICE TO READERS

Top 10 Technologies and Their Impact on CPAs does not represent an official position of the American Institute of Certified Public Accountants, and it is distributed with the understanding that the author and publisher are not rendering legal, accounting, or other professional services in this publication. If legal advice or other expert assistance is required, the services of a competent professional should be sought.

TABLE OF CONTENTS

FOREWORD

Change is inevitable, and no one should ever fear change. It means opportunity. If you can accept, adapt, and embrace the future—including its quickly evolving technology—you will be able to market yourself as a CPA who can lead his or her clients or employers into the twenty-first century.

The impact of technology on our profession will grow during the next five to ten years at a rate exponentially faster than during the past fifteen years. It is important for you to recognize and familiarize yourself with the technologies your peers identify as being the "Top 10" for 1997. They are the technologies that will have the greatest influence on all CPAs during the coming months. They affect how and when information is created, processed, stored, communicated, acquired, refined, and interpreted. They will change the way you work. They will change the way your clients and employers look to you to add value to information.

This book gives you the needed basics so you can retool yourself to keep up with the rapidly evolving technology and the resulting client needs. There is no questioning the concept that we are becoming more dependent on information systems—*technology*—that rely on little or no human intervention. But there is a limit to what the masterpieces of technology—computers and their related software—can do. You, the CPA, will have to take on the role of consultant, navigator, distiller, analyzer, and interpreter of data. You will have to become the information architect or information professional to bring your clients and employers into the information age. This is the time to grasp the opportunity.

Barry Melancon, President
American Institute of CPAs

SECURITY

technology 1

There is no shortage of sensational headlines in articles reporting security breaches of computer systems:

"*Air Force Web Site Shut as Hackers Gain Access, Change Files:* Hackers . . . broke into the site. . . shut down 80 other sites. . . put pornography pictures on our site."[1]

"*Cops Versus Robbers in Cyberspace:* . . . $15 billion loss to the U.S. software industry due to illegal copying . . ."[2]

"*Hack Attack: Cyberthieves Siphon Millions from U.S. Firms:* . . . losses due to hacking, bribery and . . . industrial espionage . . ."[3]

"*Electronic Vandals Tamper with Web Pages:* Graffiti artists . . . Web pages defaced . . . blatant mischief or malice . . ."[4]

It's no wonder that CPAs voted security as the top technology issue affecting their profession. The objective of keeping the wrong people *out* and the right people *in* your organization's computer systems is increasingly challenging.

Several factors over the last few years have contributed to skyrocketing losses from breached security. The trend of companies networking an increasing number of computers has given individuals access to more information than ever before. As companies use technology and change their organizations accordingly, a large number of individuals are being displaced through layoffs. Some of the laid-off workers have grudges large enough to incite crimes against their old organizations. And for the employees lucky enough to remain after the layoffs, loyalty is at an all time low.

Giving employees access to the Internet increases the complexity of networks and increases the chances of unwanted intruders. Some companies do not even know when uninvited hackers infiltrate their networks. Many breaches go undetected because network administrators do not monitor the traffic or do not have the right tools. Even if a company was aware of a security breach, it might not report the activity. Companies are concerned with adverse publicity concerning these intrusions.

Information systems managers have their hands full. Two surveys show that about half of the survey participants, mostly large firms, experienced an information security breach during 1996.[5,6] A recent survey by Ernst & Young shows that a whopping 78 percent of the companies surveyed incurred losses due to breached information security and disaster recovery. The largest cause of the losses was from those pesky, unwanted viruses.[7]

The first part of this chapter describes today's threats to computer systems. The next part of the chapter is about prevention. All companies should have a comprehensive information security policy that addresses (1) mundane yet crucial areas such as backups and disaster recovery and (2) the use of high-profile penetration-prevention tools such as firewalls and encryption.

The last section of this chapter presents two more topics related to security: software piracy and consumer privacy, the latter of which includes a discussion of "cookies" (bits of files containing information about website visits).

■ ■ ■
THREATS TO INFORMATION SECURITY

The most common threats to corporate information systems are—

   1. Viruses.
   2. Computer crime caused by
      a. Employees.
      b. Hackers.
      c. Competitors.
   3. Natural and man-made disasters.

FIGURE 1.1: LOSSES DUE TO INFORMATION SECURITY AND DISASTER RECOVERY

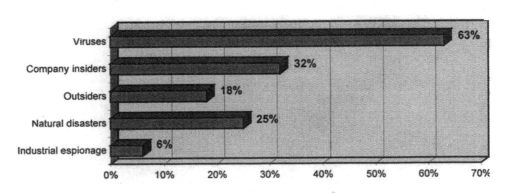

Viruses

No one wants to get a virus on his or her computer. Viruses are programs that we do not invite into our computer systems, but they crash the party anyway. Often, when they run, they do nothing. But sometimes they wreak severe damage to files and data on our computers by deleting work or rendering it unusable. Who writes viruses? I'm sure there are dozens of theories on the answer to that question, but the bottom line is that they are criminals. Writing viruses that destroy data is a crime.

1996 was a busy year for viruses. New, damaging viruses, such as the *Word.concept* (Word macro) strains and the *Hare* (as in Hare Krishna) virus, made headlines and spread faster than viruses had ever spread before, with networks and the Internet speeding the contagion.[8] 1996 was also a busy year for antivirus software. The guys and gals in the antivirus software labs kept up with the maddening pace of new viruses. They used sophisticated "bloodhounds", such as neural networks, that could sniff out and snuff out brand new viruses before they spread.[9] 1996 was a busy year for companies that suffered losses from computer viruses: the total was expected to reach between $2 billion and $3 billion.[10]

How do companies' systems get infected with viruses? The most common source of a virus infection is diskettes. Viruses hide in files on diskettes that we carry from machine to machine. Viruses can also hide in email. Infected email is a relatively new source of worry for companies because of the creation of the Word.concept virus in 1995.[11]

FIGURE 1.2: SOURCES OF VIRUSES

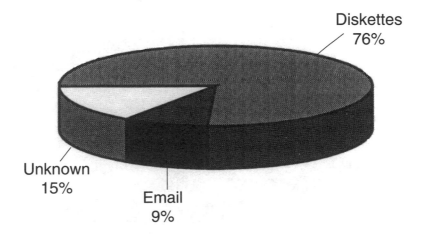

Diskettes 76%

Unknown 15%

Email 9%

Companies that have suffered from virus attacks have reported losses in productivity, losses in the use of PCs, and losses of data.[12]

Only a small percentage of viruses actually damages data. The Word.concept virus is by far the most common virus that appears now, occurring in 49 percent of all virus incidents.[13] Of the dozen or so mutations of this virus, only a few of them corrupt or destroy data. One strain converts Microsoft Word document files into document-template files and renders them basically useless. Others display a message or freeze a system. PCs at a weekly newspaper "caught" the *Wazzu Word macro* strain last year, shutting down production for two days. The virus did not destroy data, but did cause a great deal of disruption.[14] Antivirus software is effective against the Word.concept virus.

The Hare virus is particularly evil. It strikes on August 22 and September 22, displays the message "HDEuthanasia", and proceeds to overwrite hard disk files. Another version of macro viruses called *ExcelMacro.Laroux* infects Microsoft Excel spreadsheets and can travel via email.[15]

Although the vast majority of viruses do not destroy data, they can be just as disruptive to productivity. Another "form" of virus that drains productivity is the rumored virus, or hoax virus. These viruses do not exist but somehow a rumor has circulated about their upcoming appearance. Reports of hoax viruses are becoming increasingly common. Information systems personnel must investigate each report, zapping precious resources. Some of the viruses that do not exist have names and have been circulating for years: the *Good Times* virus, the *Deeyenda* virus, and the *Irina* virus

FIGURE 1.3: LOSSES DUE TO VIRUSES (MULTIPLE RESPONSES)

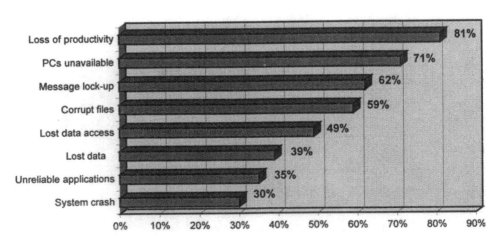

(which was a marketing stunt). Reports that a *Ghost.exe* virus will destroy a hard disk are false: it is a screen saver that is activated on a Friday the thirteenth.[16]

Until the creation of the macro viruses, the most common type of destructive virus was a boot sector virus, named for the part of the computer system it infects. The boot sector contains the commands that the computer sees when it is turned on and is especially vulnerable to an attack.[17] Companies' prevention programs must take into account this type of virus, which is detected by periodically scanning the boot sector of the computer. A scan of all files on a hard disk will reveal other types of viruses, and a scan of email files will detect even other types of viruses.

Computer Crime

The frequency of losses due to theft of proprietary information has surged in the last three or four years. A survey from the American Society for Industrial Security (ASIS) describes what types of information are commonly targeted:

- Strategic plans
- Research and development information
- Manufacturing processes
- Marketing plans
- Intellectual property
- Financial data
- Merger/acquisition data
- Customer lists
- Personnel plans[18]

The most common breach of information occurs not by computer systems break-ins, but over the telephone. An outsider will call an employee and get the information sought by acting like someone else. Figure 1.4 presents how information is stolen, based on the ASIS survey.[19]

In this section, we'll discuss the classes of individuals most likely to perform computer crimes. The list includes—

- Employees, ex-employees, and other trusted parties
- U.S. and foreign competitors
- Hackers[20]

Figure 1.4: How Information Is Stolen in Companies

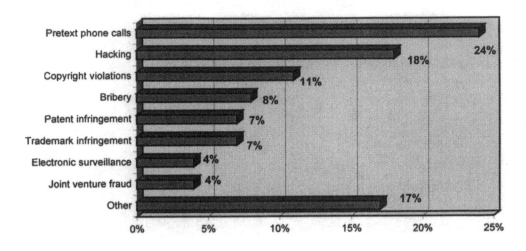

Figure 1.5: Employees Take the Largest Piece of the Pie in Stolen Corporate Information

Who is stealing proprietary information?

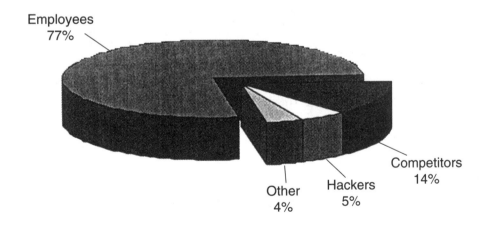

Employees

Believe it or not, one of the most damaging enemies to corporate information lurks inside corporate walls. Seventy-seven percent of information is taken by employees and other trusted parties.[21] Frank Clark, a criminal investigator who once cracked a murder case from evidence stored on a hard disk, puts that percentage a little higher. He says that 80 percent to 85 percent of computer crime losses are inside jobs.[22]

William Gaede, who worked for Intel, tried to download files that contained the blueprint for the Intel Pentium chip. He couldn't because of security limitations. But he could display the blueprints on his computer screen. He then proceeded to videotape them. He left the United States with the videos and was arrested for transportation of stolen property and mail fraud.[23]

In some people's minds, computer crimes do not seem as serious as other physical crimes, like breaking into a building. In the comfort of home or office, a person can "peek" into a confidential file or email. The same person would not dare steal a car or break into a house, but might be tempted to read a private email or sift through unauthorized files.[24]

What types of employee engage in these acts? It's not always easy to identify them, but Frank Clark lists some common traits. These employees typically—

- Are low wage earners with little or no investment in the business.
- Spend a lot of time on the computer.
- Sometimes exceed their authority.
- Might have a grudge from losing a promotion or from some other work-related disappointment.[25]

With the waves of downsizing occurring in the last decade, there are armies of former and current employees who have lost their drive to be loyal and who might have just enough of a grudge to act when the situation arises. Ernst & Young warns against keeping terminated employees on-site as a result of relocation package benefits that include the use of an office for a period of time. One disgruntled employee is all it takes to impart considerable damage to corporate information.[26]

Competitors

It is easy to obtain information on your competitors without breaking any laws. A company's Web site is a good first stop. But for a few companies, that's not enough. The number of incidents of companies stealing information from their competitors is higher for cutthroat industries, such as high technology. Industries with large contracts that involve a bidding process in which millions or billions of dollars are at stake are ripe for this type of crime.

One notorious case between competitors Borland and Symantec lasted four years before it was resolved in late 1996. Eugene Wang, a Borland employee, allegedly supplied Symantec with Borland's product marketing plans. Then he went to work for Symantec. Borland filed suit against Symantec.[27] The case never reached trial because of a questionable $13,000 contribution from Borland to the district attorney's office and other legal issues. It was dismissed in November 1996, primarily because of its loss of relevance due both to the age of the dispute and to changes in California law.[28]

Another case involved two competitors, Cadence and Avant!, that sold systems that designed integrated circuits. It started with a Cadence engineer who acted suspiciously during his last days of work. When the police raided the engineer's apartment, they supposedly found source code owned by Cadence. Later, a Cadence employee who helped a customer that ran both Avant! and Cadence products noticed a programming bug in the Avant! software that was identical to one in the Cadence software. The police confiscated Avant!'s files and programs, and Cadence filed suit against Avant! for copyright infringement. Avant! filed against Cadence for damaging its business reputation.[29]

It is not unusual for employees to be "double agents" at some companies where multibillion dollar bids are at stake. An employee of Company A, who is really working for Company B, can provide Company B with valuable details about how Company A is bidding. A coincidence when two bids come in only $1,000 apart? You be the judge.

Hackers

A small percentage of our population is made up of criminals. They rob grocery stores and gas stations; they sell drugs; they may commit worse crimes. Some criminals came with us into cyberspace: these people are called hackers. They are the criminals of the computer world. They rob companies of information, compromise systems, and perform fraudulent acts. The most common things hackers do, according to a survey by WarRoom Research LLC, are listed below:[30]

- Probe/scan systems—   14.6%
- Compromise email or other documents—   12.6%
- Introduce virus—   10.6%
- Compromise trade secrets—   9.8%
- Download data—   8.1%
- Change data—   6.8%
- Install password sniffer—   6.6%
- Deny use of service—   6.3%

Hackers can penetrate security in many ways. They can intercept Internet traffic, such as files or email. They can attempt to break into a private network. They can even reach into your own computer files from a Web site that you are visiting by using an applet that is received by your browser software. In the last case, both Microsoft Internet Explorer and Netscape Navigator allow Java, ActiveX, and other applets to run commands on your computer. Each time new security holes in the browsers are discovered, usually by the computer security teams at Princeton University, Microsoft and Netscape issue software fixes very quickly. The only way to totally prevent this possible breach is to turn off Java and ActiveX capabilities in the browsers.[31]

Hackers are generally young, in their teens or twenties. For most, hacking is a way to play pranks on people. Some see it as revenge. Others see it as a brag or a challenge: each intrusion is a "notch on the bedpost," according to a seventeen-year-old hacker from Newark, California.[32]

Hackers like to make their mark on Web sites. The site of the American Psychoanalytic Association was broken into by a hacker trying to impress his girlfriend. It took a week for the Web site of the Nation of Islam to be cleaned up after a recent attack by unidentified hackers.[33]

The government is a constant source of amusement for hackers. Over the 1996 Christmas holidays (a favorite time for hackers) the Air Force Web site was penetrated. Hackers replaced military service fact sheets and commanders' biographies with a sexually explicit video and a claim that the government lies to citizens. During summer 1996, an image of Hitler and a swastika appeared on the Department of Justice's Web site, courtesy of hackers. In autumn 1996, the Central Intelligence Agency's Web site was renamed "The Central Stupidity Agency" and garnished with adult photos.[34]

Most actions by hackers are nuisances that do not pose any real threat. But hackers have skills that should not be taken lightly. A few companies are hiring them to find holes in their security systems. Hired on as a temp, one hacker accessed the company's $1 billion project files in his first few hours on the job. He printed fake business cards, hooked up a portable Unix to its network, and forged the president's digital signature on documents. He was successful at extracting legal, licensing, and top-secret data, and built himself a trapdoor so he could return in the future.[35]

Frank Clark urges companies not to hire hackers. He says the basic nature of people is simply not going to change, and a company does not have enough skill to police hackers, even in its own environment.[36]

The attitude of the hacker community is getting scary, even to former hackers. One twenty-year-old reasons that if a network administrator who is paid $60,000 a year or more cannot keep the network secure, then the company deserves the intrusion. Other hackers just sit around formatting hard disks (this erases everything on the disk) to make people angry.[37]

Natural and Man-Made Disasters

Mother Nature can deal her hand occasionally. Whether it's a fire that wipes out one company or a hurricane that wipes out a city, corporations must protect themselves from the possibility of a disaster. Periodically, a company data center must be rebuilt because of a man-made disaster such as the Oklahoma City bombing.

In all of these cases, off-site storage and backup data centers play a major role in getting online again quickly. In one case in Oklahoma City, the off-site storage area containing backups of the company's data was across the street from the company's building. Both were damaged in the bombing. In this case, the off-site backup was not far enough away to make a difference.

In early 1997, floods in the western United States proved a challenge for some systems staff. Companies with a solid plan stayed dry. The systems personnel of The Hampton Inn in Reno, NV, placed its equipment on racks while four feet of water swept through the downtown area. The network was brought down in a normal shutdown procedure, and critical systems were moved to the designated backup site. Reservations continued to be taken and honored without a hitch.[38]

■ ■ ■
PREVENTIVE MEASURES

An Information Security Policy

Every company should adopt and enforce an information systems security policy. In 1992, 82 percent of companies had security policies, but in 1996 the percentage dropped to 54 percent.[39]

A security policy will help to clarify employee responsibility and improve awareness of security issues. It should be created at the management level with input from all levels of personnel who access corporate information. It should cover not only information in computers but access to all information in the company.

A sampling of what a security policy should cover includes—

■ Access controls, such as—
  — User IDs and passwords, including use of encryption.
  — Access to equipment.
  — Access to files, including use of encryption.
  — Access to systems.
  — Remote-access controls.
  — Network access controls.
  — Internet and external systems access, including use of firewalls (which will be explained later in this chapter).
  — Monitoring of and responses to breaches in access.

■ Roles and responsibilities, such as—
  — Employees', contractors', and temps' responsibilities.
  — Managers' responsibilities for data access restriction.
  — Systems personnel responsibilities.
  — Use of confidentiality agreements.
  — Restrictions on downloading Internet files.
  — Intellectual property treatment.
  — Privacy issues.

■ System controls, such as—
  — Prevention software, including virus scans.
  — Data center access.
  — Systems library access and change control.
  — Systems audits.
  — Data storage requirements.
  — Data purge procedures.

- Disaster recovery planning, such as—
  — Routine backups on all platforms.
  — Routine processing.
  — Off-site storage.
  — Alternate data-center site for emergency processing.
  — Communications, including emergency, training and testing.
  — Emergency configuration and critical systems identification.

The security policy should be fleshed out with guidelines in each of these major areas. As you can see, most of the policy will consist of such straightforward ideas as the following:

- Users must log off their computers when they leave their desks.
- Security guards must question all employees leaving the building with equipment.
- Users must not post their password on a sticky note near their monitor.
- Users must not bring diskettes in from other computers without running a virus scan first.
- Users should save their work often, even every few minutes.
- Users' passwords should not be easily guessed, like their dog's name or their kids' names.
- Users must guard what information they give over the phone.
- Users must back up their computer data every day.

Simply by following these guidelines, a company will solve a majority of its daily productivity-busters regarding information security. These simple guidelines should not be ignored, and employees should be trained for constant awareness and compliance.

Take the example of backups. Only 50 percent of people back up their data.[40] Many more people think the systems department does it for them. A systems department may back up certain files on a server. But if the user stores files on his or her PC's local hard drive, they may or may not be backed up. The backup policy portion of the security policy must be thorough enough to give users a good idea of what they are responsible for.

Cost versus Risk

A company will want to compare the costs of prevention with the costs and risks of the threats to its information before deciding what security measures to take. An informed company will put inexpensive preventative steps in place, such as a policy on scanning diskettes originating from outside the company to avoid the relatively high costs of being infected with viruses. A company that spends $100,000 on a firewall to prevent viruses (where a small percentage of viruses come from) but has no policy about scanning diskettes (where a vast majority of viruses come from) is not properly allocating its resources using risk management and cost-effectiveness as a basis. This happens quite frequently. A CPA who understands these statistically based decisions can be an asset in the decision-making process.

Three prevention topics will be presented here in more detail: virus prevention, encryption, and firewalls; then this section of the chapter will close with some tips for information security.

Virus Prevention

Some of the companies that sell anti-virus software are—

- Symantec Corporation, www.symantec.com/avcenter.
- IBM, www.brs.ibm.com/ibmav.html.
- McAfee Associates, www.mcafee.com.
- Command Software Systems, www.commandcom.com.
- Cheyenne Software, Inc., www.cheyenne.com/security.

Virus detection software that continuously runs is the best prevention. Information-security employees should install the antivirus software on client machines as well as on server machines for full protection. Because new viruses are written daily, it is important to upgrade the anti-virus software every thirty to sixty days so that it can detect the newer viruses. The most convenient method for updating is using the software vendor's Web site, where a patch (an up-to-date software program file) is usually available for downloading.

For companies that take preventive steps, the cost of virus attacks are greatly reduced. According to the National Computer Security Administration, the cost of virus attacks per one thousand PCs varies depending on how much corporations protect themselves:

- If no preventive steps are taken, computer viruses will cost a company $1.8 million.
- If basic steps, such as an employee awareness program, are implemented, the costs are reduced to $800,000.
- If the company runs daily virus scanners on half of the PCs, the costs are further reduced to $400,000.
- If the company runs full-time background scanners on half of the PCs, the costs are just $30,000.[41]

A few companies have set up central help desks to handle virus activity. Employees can call and receive guidance if they suspect their PC is infected. Quick response by a trained team can greatly reduce a company's exposure and downtime.

The war is waged in virus-detection labs around the country. The tools have become quite sophisticated. IBM uses neural networks to detect new viruses; it unleashes them on the Web, and they track down code sequences that look the same as virus code sequences. Symantec's "spider" randomly downloads files from around the Internet and checks them for viruses. The spider also keeps its eyes on five hundred sites known for previously downloading viruses.[42]

Seven Locks Software, Inc. in Bethesda, Maryland, takes a new approach with a product called SWAT—Secure Web Anti-Virus Technology, which can be downloaded free from http://www.sevenlocks.com. Users can scan their systems as often as they want. If a virus is found, Seven Locks charges $5 to clean up the virus, if the user wishes. You don't pay unless your PC is sick and you wish to have the antidote.[43]

In 1997, IBM plans to install a system over the Internet that will allow programs to capture and isolate viruses on users' PCs, and to develop and deliver an antidote within a few minutes.[44]

Encryption, Digital Certificates, and Digital Signatures

Encryption can be used to encode information such as passwords, messages, and company files. The recipient of the encoded information must use a "key" (which is like a password) to decode it. In public key cryptography, there are two keys, a public key and a private key. The public key is widely known but the private key is secret to the user. A person wishing to send an encrypted message can encrypt the data using a person's public key. The recipient can then decrypt it with his or her private key.

CPAs who send client files or sensitive company information over the Internet or a public network should encrypt files. Email can be encrypted as well.

Three popular packages make encryption of sensitive data easy:

1. *Symantic's Your Eyes Only* is very popular with businesses and available in software and office supply stores.

2. *McAfee's PC Crypto* is also available in retail outlets.

3. Pretty Good Privacy, Inc. offers a DOS-based product, *PGP*, that is popular with Internet users. The Windows version is still "vaporware" as of this writing, although an email encryption product is available and runs on a Windows platform. Visit http://www.pgp.com for the latest in product offerings by Pretty Good Privacy.

Digital certificates provide a way to authenticate the person who made the transaction or created a document. They are electronic identifications and

FIGURE 1.6: McAFEE's PC CRYPTO SOFTWARE

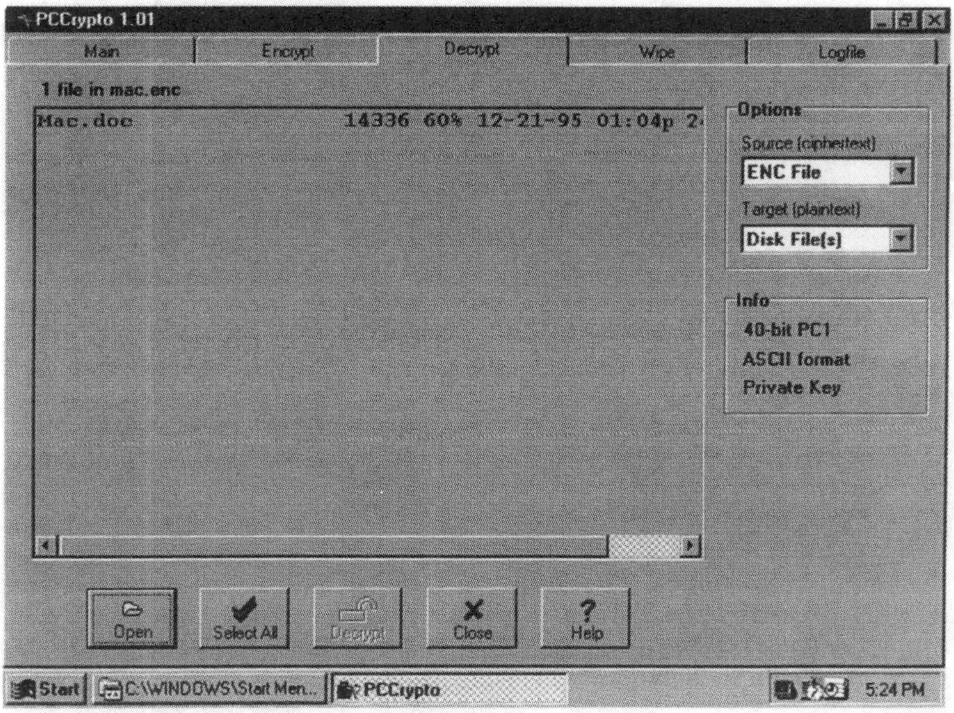

perform a function similar to driver's licenses. Digital certificates are encrypted with a public and a private key.

Digital signatures help to authenticate the originator of the document. They also ensure that the attached message is intact and hasn't been tampered with. Digital signatures are encrypted with a public and a private key as well.[45]

Data Encryption Standard (DES)

Data Encryption Standard (DES) is the most widely used encryption standard. The algorithm is used in point-of-sale machines, computers that transfer funds, and automated teller machines (ATMs). DES encryption has never been "cracked." However, today's computers are growing in power and can crack passwords and keys that are short. DES's 56-bit key length is considered too short by some who are calling for a 75-bit key length. The longer key length would be statistically harder to crack because of the increase in possible combinations of values. The cost to the banking industry to comply with a new standard would be enormous.[46]

Secure Sockets Layer (SSL)

Secure Sockets Layer (SSL) is a widely used encryption standard for doing business on the Web. Business transactions can be encrypted when the individual is using a compatible browser, such as Netscape Navigator, Secure Mosaic, or Microsoft Internet Explorer, and the business is using a secure server. In the Netscape Navigator browser, you can tell if you are in a secure server if the key on the bottom left corner of the screen is in one piece. It will be broken, or in two pieces, if you are in part of the Internet that is not secure. Similarly, in Microsoft Internet Explore, you can tell if you are in a secure server when a padlock appears in the bottom right corner of your screen. You should not give your credit card number over the Internet unless you see a solid key in Netscape or a padlock in Internet Explorer.

Secure Electronic Transaction (SET)

Secure Electronic Transaction (SET) is a protocol for processing credit card transactions over the Internet. It checks the identity of each party in the transaction through signed, unforgeable certificates and maintains privacy by allowing only necessary transaction information to go to each party. Netscape, Microsoft, Visa and MasterCard are responsible for creating the

SET standard so that the credit card transaction processing software will be compatible.

The SET protocol will not be completely tested until late 1997. However, some vendors, such as Wells Fargo, are jumping ahead and developing software based on the SET standard as it stands to date. Wells Fargo announced in December 1996 that it will offer digital certificates based on the SET standard.[47]

Secure Hypertext Transfer Protocol (SHTTP)

Secure Hypertext Transfer Protocol (SHTTP) is a secure version of the Web access protocol, Hypertext Transfer Protocol (HTTP), that utilized digital signatures to authenticate identity in electronic transactions.

Firewalls

A company that has network access to the Internet probably needs a firewall. Firewalls provide a barrier between the company's private network and any public networks, including the Internet, that the company accesses. A firewall offers the security to keep uninvited individuals from viewing sensitive corporate information.

Physically, a firewall can consist of hardware, software, or both, as is the usual case. Firewalls can be purchased from vendors or built internally. Companies that need firewalls should determine their business requirements before shopping for one, just as they would with any hardware or software purchase. For example, a company should make sure it can easily monitor network traffic and be able to determine patterns of access that could be preludes to break-ins. The general features of a firewall include:

- Support of common Internet services, such as mail, Web access, file download, and newsgroup access.
- Support of all necessary hardware and operating system platforms.
- Prevention of unauthorized access to internal networks, including session monitoring and alerting, activity reporting and logging facility.
- Authentication of remote-access users
- Flexibility to define exceptions and thresholds
- Ease of use and installation

- Audit capabilities
- Technical support of the product by the vendor, twenty-four hours a day

Firewalls are good for companies with one or both of the following requirements—

1. Companies with direct access to the Internet or other external networks can use them to control access between company networks and the external networks.

2. Companies wishing to control access internally between department networks can use firewalls for this purpose.

The security provided by firewall products varies greatly. A company should thoroughly question the security features of any product that it is considering for purchase. If it is not secure enough, the company should walk away from the purchase, advises Jeffrey Schiller, a network manager for the Massachusetts Institute of Technology and a security area director for the Internet Engineering Task Force. Only then will vendors consider developing more secure products.[48]

After a firewall purchase, the firewall installation is critical. A systems person trained in both security systems and network systems is the best choice as a firewall installer. A firewall that is installed incorrectly has plenty of penetrable holes and provides a false sense of security to managers who think their data are safe.[49]

Tips for Making Information Secure

1. Understand that network administrators are not necessarily security experts.

2. Uninstall features of a network that you do not use. Eliminating unused programs will reduce complexity and do away with additional entry points into a system.[50]

3. Agree on a centralized encryption policy that specifies keys are stored on a central machine so there is more control over work done by employees who leave the company.

4. Provide extra attention to policies relating to laptops and remote users. Because of laptop theft, which is frequent, users with sensitive data on laptops should not use automated log-on routines, but should use password protected or other

secure log-on routines. For example, do not choose the "save password" option at log-on. Then, you (or a burglar) will be required to key in your password each time you log into your system. Sensitive files should be encrypted to further thwart burglars.[51]

5. Require all employees, contractors, and temps to sign a confidentiality agreement.

6. Delete inactive user IDs and keep access controls up-to-date. Users should have access to data and systems on a need-to-know basis, with approvals by department managers.

7. Classify data by importance and ownership. Access controls, encryption, and file passwords should be implemented accordingly.[52]

■ ■ ■
COPYRIGHT PROTECTION

It's a problem in the entertainment industry; it's a problem in the software industry; and it's an increasing problem on the Internet. Whether it's CDs, videos, software packages, or Web pages, people are illegally copying and distributing music, movies, software, and information that isn't theirs to distribute.

The problem has caused companies to lose billions of dollars and is forcing some people off the Internet. Comedian Dave Barry stopped posting his weekly column on the Internet last year because it was so widely copied.[53] The ability to click and save Web graphics and quickly download files has made the Internet a breeding ground for copyright violations.

Software piracy, or illegally copying software, amounts to a $15 billion industry, estimates the Business Software Alliance.[54] The Software Publishers Association puts the figure at $13.2 billion for 1995. Of all the software used in 1995, 46 percent was obtained illegally.[55] Those of us who pay for our software are paying higher prices because of the people who do not pay at all.

Much of the theft results from organized, high-volume thieves who mass-distribute the pirated versions. But a lot of the problem results from individuals who simply do not understand, or decide to ignore, software licensing agreements. Although licenses vary, most licenses allow the software to be installed and used on only one machine. That means if you put the software on four machines, you should buy four copies. Some business owners look at me as though I'm crazy when I tell them that.

It should be the job of the network administrator to track a firm's software inventory. Periodic compliance audits are good ideas. Fines are hefty if a company is caught violating copyright laws. The corporate security policy should include a section on copyright law enforcement, which should cover software piracy as well as Internet-content copying and file downloads. Just as stealing a car is theft, stealing software is a serious crime.

Vendors have not been blind to copyright problems on the Internet. Some products under development that are planned to counter piracy include—

- Cryptolopes, which are cryptography envelopes that will wrap around copyrighted files for distribution or purchase. They can't be opened without a key.
- Digital watermarks, which will be embedded in pictures or text and will identify the author of the document.[56]

■ ■ ■

PRIVACY

Internet Privacy

When phone directories were first posted on the Internet, privacy advocates heightened the debate about information privacy. The phone directory in question posted judges, prosecutors, and police officers' unlisted numbers, putting some individuals in danger of being easily found by enemies made in their work lives.[57] The question of privacy will continue as hard-to-get information becomes globally available on the Internet.

The privacy debate climaxed again in 1996 when a major research database company posted a list of names on the Internet that included Social Security numbers. The list was quickly withdrawn amid loud opposition to the posting.

The Internet privacy debate will most likely be kept in check by strong consumer desires for privacy, although individual incidents will continue.

Cookies

Last time you surfed the Internet, chances are you were followed. By a "cookie". The next time you visit a Web site, the Web site may deposit a little remembrance of your visit on your own hard disk. These cookies are bits of files that contain information about your visit to a Web site. Cookies leave trails of information for the Web site programs so that when you visit the site again, you will be remembered. Companies like them because they can track how often you visit the Web site and how long you stay.

You can look into your own cookie file to see what sites have deposited the little goodies on your hard disk. For Netscape users, you can find a cookies.txt file in c:\programs\netscape\navigator for Windows users or ~/.netscape/cookies for Unix users. Mac users can look in their System Folder under Preferences: Netscape. Microsoft Internet Explorer users can look for files in c:\windows\cookies.[58]

You can set your browser to alert you if a site is depositing cookies on your system. In Microsoft Internet Explorer, choose *View, Options,*

FIGURE 1.7: COOKIES ON THE AUTHOR'S HARD DISK

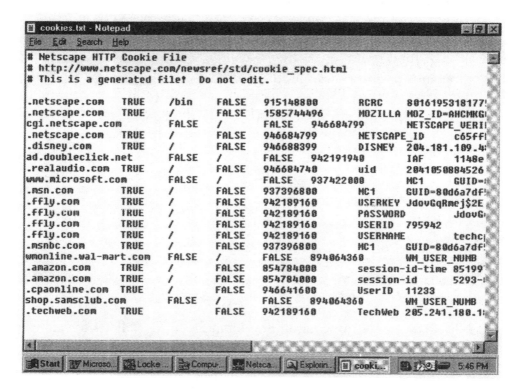

Advanced, and *Warn before accepting cookies.* In Netscape Navigator, choose *Options, Network Preferences, Protocols,* and *Show an alert before accepting a cookie.*

If you do not like the idea of cookies, you can delete them. If you delete them, do not expect a Web site to "recognize" you on a subsequent visit. Deleting cookie files will protect your privacy between Web sessions but not during them. A new product, the PGPcookiecutter by Pretty Good Privacy, Inc., will protect you from cookies during Web sessions by blocking them and allowing you to surf anonymously.

Email Privacy

If you write and send an email that vents about how bad your boss is, the recipient will read it, the network administrator could read it, and the email systems programmers could read it. Chances are your boss will get wind of it too. Company email was never meant to be private. Security policies and procedures manuals should include a section on the use of email. It was never meant to distribute recipes or restaurant reviews. It was never meant to manage the football pool. A company policy should be clear on what email can and cannot be used for.

Email can be used as a weapon or a time-waster. I talked about these problems in a recent conversation with Charles Richardson, Director of Quality Assurance, and Sam Hodge, Information Specialist Coordinator, both at Internet America, Inc., a regional ISP. An enemy can send thousands of email messages to your box, and you have to deal with them. This is called "spamming". Sending a large email can clog your box or bring down an entire network. It's probably a good idea to try to stay off advertiser's lists as well, so that you minimize the amount of unsolicited email that you receive. Avoid filling out personal information at Web sites that you visit, and watch where you leave your name in cyberspace. Online services encourage unhappy customers to report violators sending unsolicited email to your online service mail box.

■ ■ ■

CPAs and Security

There are many opportunities for CPAs in the area of information security. CPAs can be instrumental in developing security policies for companies and advising executives about information security risks. Also, security naturally relates to assurance services.

Many management consulting services are being offered in the area of security. The many facets of security range from disaster recovery to copyright protection to computer fraud. CPAs who are deeply interested in this topic have several areas of study to choose from.

CPAs are in the business of providing information. Protecting the information they provide is paramount. It is little wonder that security is the number one technology issue this year.

IMAGE PROCESSING

technology 2

Now where is that file? Let's see, I know I had it Friday, but then Sharon needed it. I'll check to see if she still has it. "Hey Sharon, how was your weekend? . . . Oh, by the way, do you have the Stinson file?"

"Not anymore. I gave it to Bruce."

"Hey Bruce, how was your weekend? . . . Oh, by the way, do you have the Stinson file?"

"Not anymore. I gave it to Liz."

"Hey Liz, how was your weekend?" . . .

Dialogues like this probably go on in your office all the time. It's the constant paper chase. When two or three team members are working on the same client project, they also need the same files. And they go around and around searching for the exact document they need. Some workers spend as much as 30 percent of their time looking for documents. CPA George Strickland says it costs about $150 to retrieve a misplaced document.[1]

How can we get more productive in our handling of paper? The answer lies in the technology that CPAs voted number two in our profession, falling from the number one post in 1996. Image processing is the conversion of paper documents to electronic images.

Image processing brings us closer to the realization of the paperless office. It's often mentioned in the same sentence as electronic document management (EDM), which is a broad category that includes the automation of many business functions around electronic documents. Basic functions of an EDM system will include document capture, storage, and retrieval.

Work flow is another related function that is often mentioned with document management and image processing. We'll defer our discussion of work flow until Technology 8.

This chapter describes the functions and features of EDM systems, with a focus on image processing. The following topics are presented:

1. The business case for imaging systems
2. Common features and functions
3. Audit considerations and implications
4. Future issues and trends

■ ■ ■
The Business Case for Imaging Systems

All Size Companies Can Benefit

Companies both large and small are saving big by implementing imaging systems. Several changes in the last decade are driving the savings. Costs of imaging systems, as with most technology solutions, have plummeted in the last decade. Imaging technology is available on desktop, so small companies can easily benefit from imaging today.

At the budget-basement level, a sole proprietor or mom-and-pop operation can buy a scanner and some indexing software and have a primitive but functional electronic filing system. At the high end, a Fortune 100 company can spend millions to automate one or more of its accounting functions and fully integrate imaging, workflow, and transaction-processing systems. Everywhere in between these two extremes, companies are benefiting from imaging.

One East Coast CPA scans in every paper memo he receives, then he throws away the paper. He can look up everything online. He even takes his scanner with him when he travels. Carrying the laptop and the scanner is a lot lighter than stacks of paper, he says.

Eric McMillen, a systems consultant with Boomer Consulting, helped a regional CPA firm with a project that streamlined tax preparation and document storage. At the CPA firm, while a client was meeting with the tax partner, the client's tax working papers were scanned in, and the originals were returned to the client before he left the office. The imaging and workflow systems saved the firm $75,000 in paper costs, according to the firm's CEO.

At Alliant Foodservice Inc., Mike Noble, finance director, cut his accounts payable staff from several hundred to thirty-five with an imaging system from FileNet Corporation, one of the industry leaders. For $5 million, Noble purchased OSCAR (Filenet's Online Scanning and Retrieval), which now scans and indexes six thousand invoices a day. Alliant, a $4.5 billion food service distributor, won an award in 1995 for best imaging application from the Giga Information Group.[2]

Total 1995 revenue for imaging, workflow, and document-management software was as follows:[3]

1. Imaging— $820 million
2. Workflow— $661 million
3. Document-management— $181 million

A Multiproduct Solution

Often an imaging solution will be made up of several hardware and software products from different vendors. Sometimes the component parts do not fit together seamlessly. Document-management products are better integrated than they have been in the past, but there is still a long way to go in this area. In fact, the topic of EDM can mean different things to different vendors. To the novice, the differences in product features can be daunting and expensive if misunderstood. Value-added resellers (VARs) and consultants are common in the computer industry, and many companies feel better hiring these integrators to choose and implement the system that is right for their company. All companies considering purchases of document-management systems should become thoroughly educated in the technology before signing any contracts.

Rolex is satisfied with its multivendors solution, which includes Compaq Computer Corporation workstations running Microsoft Windows, a Novell Inc. optical server, Hewlett-Packard Company optical-disk jukeboxes (storage devices), Diamond Head Software Inc. imaging tools, and a custom-designed Synergetix system. A watch-repair technician can quickly view twenty years of repair records for any particular customer or watch.[4]

For its imaging and workflow applications, a Midwest CPA firm chose Watermark Enterprise Imaging Software (which runs on Windows NT Server), a Bell and Howell High-Speed Scanner, and a Hewlett-Packard optical-storage jukebox.

Types of Applications

Service companies that operate paper-intensive processes are naturals for an imaging system. Insurance claims processing, bank loan applications, and accounting systems are common examples of systems that greatly benefit from imaging. Colonial Savings, a Fort Worth bank, implemented a system from ViewStar that allowed online lookup of its thirty thousand loans. Frank Manci, coordinator of the imaging project, says customers receive instant answers instead of waiting two days, and loan officers are "raving" about the system and how it has changed their lives.[5]

The Westinghouse Savannah River Company, which is a nuclear components contractor for the Department of Energy, has millions of documents stored in a three-hundred-square-mile facility in South Carolina. It is building its own imaging system using three pieces of software as the base:

1. RSA Data Security's encryption software
2. Documentum's Enterprise Document Management System
3. Adobe's Acrobat and Capture software

When finished, the system will allow the twelve thousand employees to view information from databases, Microsoft Office documents, engineering drawings, company policies and procedures, technical documents, and more. It expects to save 10 percent in labor productivity and 25 percent in storage costs after project completion.[6]

Universities are getting into the act. The Physical Plant Department of the University of North Carolina has thousands of forms from contractors, regulatory agencies, and utility companies as well as internally generated documents to track and manage. It has implemented an image processing system using Keyfile imaging and workflow software, magnetic media for documents in progress, and WORM (write once read many) optical storage technology for archiving documents. The fifty-five users on Windows workstations and a Novell network can retrieve, file, distribute, fax, email, annotate, and destroy documents in the system.[7]

Budget Rent-a-Car scans and indexes its accounts payable documents, which are used in a workflow system. The system matches invoices and purchase orders, and is integrated with its mainframe accounts payable system by Walker Interactive Systems. Using the FileNet workflow system and optical storage, the company has reduced its cycle time from five days to two, reduced its headcount by 35 percent, and increased its productivity by 30 percent.[8]

CPA firms are turning to image processing in droves. A Miami firm is putting hand scanners on every professional's desk so that tax documents can be scanned into a central repository. The firm chose Watermark imaging software and CD-R (compact disc-recordable) storage technology for its imaging system.

Another CPA firm is taking a completely different track and imaging only older files. It is using WORM optical storage technology and a simple indexing method. It recouped its $12,500 investment in the first year by reducing its rental space.[9]

Benefits

The benefits of imaging systems include—

- Reduced storage costs, such as expenditures for—
  — Filing cabinets.
  — Office or warehouse rent (less square footage is needed).
  — Labor.
- Improved productivity from reductions in—
  — Time spent searching for documents.
  — Misfiled or lost documents.
  — Copying of originals that two people need at once.
- Improved management and control through—
  — Consistent, automated processes that eliminate human errors.
  — Improved access controls.

Risks

Although there are hundreds of success stories with image processing applications, there are a few casualties, too. Most of these can be prevented by understanding and managing the risks associated with these projects.

The largest reason for failure is not technical in nature, but human. Human resistance to a new system or procedure is always very strong in any type of technology project. With imaging, people must give up a basic component of business: their papers. That's pretty scary for some people. Managers can prevent this type of failure by—

1. Involving all levels of staff at the very beginning of the project.
2. Communicating the business benefits of the system to all participants.
3. Providing thorough training on the system.
4. Supporting and encouraging the use of the system until the system becomes a normal part of the business routine.

Another reason that imaging systems fail is their lack of integration with the rest of the company systems. For some business applications, such as a law library or a tax library, integration is not that important, and a stand-alone imaging system could succeed. But for other systems, such as a loan application process, integration with other systems becomes paramount to the success of the project. Companies that do not initially plan for integration but want to add it later should include that requirement in the planning phase of the project.

One more major reason for failure of an imaging system is a lack of proper disaster-recovery planning. The company must grasp that the imaging system now contains valuable company documents that must be preserved and protected against probable losses. Planning for disaster recovery in an imaging system is even more important if the company decides to destroy original records.

Requirements

Companies wishing to install imaging systems must answer several questions, a few of which are listed below.

- What are the overall goals of the system?
- What documents will be imaged?
  - What types of documents can the software handle?
  - What access controls and requirements does the company need, and what does the software provide?
  - What storage requirements and features does the company need, and what does the software offer?
- Will the company start imaging documents produced today, one year ago, or ten years ago?
- What security features are needed by the company and provided by software?
- Will there be remote users?
- Should the imaging system be integrated with other systems and, if so, which ones?
- Will the original documents be destroyed after scanning? What are the related legal and procedural issues of destroying documents?
- What backup and disaster-recovery techniques will be used in case of systems failure?

Vendors

There are about a hundred vendors that provide products in this field. Additionally, there are a few hundred VARs that act as integrators. A novice can find the choices confusing, as different products offer different features, features overlap other products, or features fall short of integration possibilities. Some of the vendors include the following:

FileNet owns both Saros and Watermark and offers several products. It is considered the market leader. Watermark Enterprise Series is popular with CPAs and is a Windows- and Windows NT-based document-imaging system that is integrated with Microsoft Back Office.

Wang offers OPENImage and also OPENWorkflow, and has agreements with PC DOCS and Microsoft.

ViewStar offers a product called ViewStar that is very flexible and can be developed rapidly.

Optika offers File Power and Power Flow, good for inexperienced users.

Keyfile offers a product called Keyfile and is also good for inexperienced users.

A good benchmark study that compares these and more products can be found at the Web site of the Association for Information and Image Management International (AIIM) (http://www.aiim.org). The study was done by Doculabs and the University of Illinois, Chicago.[10]

■ ■ ■

FEATURES AND FUNCTIONS OF EDM SYSTEMS

An EDM system will contain at least the following basic features:

- Document capture
- Document storage
- Document retrieval

We'll discuss each one.

Document Capture

Scanners

Documents can be captured by a scanner or created electronically by word processing, email, or other desktop systems. There are many types of scanners, ranging from low-end handheld scanners, to the popular flatbed

FIGURE 2.1: THE AIIM INTERNATIONAL WEB SITE

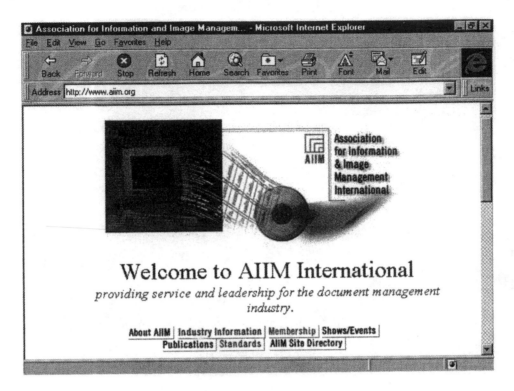

scanners, to high-volume customized machines. Scanners work somewhat like fax machines, reading the dark and light areas on a page and digitizing the image so that it can be stored in a graphic format. Even text is stored in a graphic image unless it is further processed by OCR (optical character recognition) software.

Several features of a scanner should be considered before purchase. Questions your firm should ask include the following:

- How many documents can the scanner process per minute?
- What size paper will it scan?
- What is the scanning resolution?
- How large are the image files? Is a compression routine used?
- For high-volume operations, are there autofeed and dual-sided processing capabilities?
- Can color images be processed?

There are many excellent scanners on the market for all size operations. Table 2.1 lists several vendors as a starting point:[11]

TABLE 2.1: SCANNER VENDORS

High-end	Eastman Kodak Co.	$80,000 to $100,000
	ScanOptics, Inc.	$150,000 and up
Midrange	Hewlett-Packard	Approximately $3,000 for the 4SI
	Fujitsu	$5,000 to $10,000
	Ricoh Corp.	$6,400 for the IS420
Low-end	Bayer Corp. (Afga)	$1,000 to $3,000
	Canon	$700
	Epson	$800 to $1300
	Hewlett-Packard	$1,000 for the 4C
	Logitek Microtek Lab, Inc.	$200 to $2,000
	Ricoh Corp.	$600 for the CS–300
	Tamarac Technologies, Inc.	$500 to $700
	Umax Technologies, Inc.	$800
	Visioneer, Inc.	$300

In addition to their use for imaging, scanners can serve many other business functions, among them the following:

- Photographs and drawings can be scanned into documents for newsletter production, marketing brochures, Web site use, presentations, and reports.

- Paper clutter on desktops can be scanned in even though most of this paper is not important enough to be cataloged or stored as part of the imaging system.

Some companies will place a scanner on every employee's desktop. More likely, companies will have centralized scanning stations or a few networked scanners. Companies that network their computers should consider the impact on network traffic: scanners can be a drain on bandwidth.

Optical Character Recognition (OCR)/Intelligent Character Recognition (ICR)

Optical Character Recognition (OCR) is the technology that takes scanning a step further by converting the scanned graphic images into a searchable text format. Take the example of scanning in a letter you receive in the mail. When scanned, the letter is most likely stored in a bitmap image format that can be read only by a graphics program. The OCR process converts the bitmap image into a text format that can be read and edited by any of the popular word processing programs.

Section by section, and piece by piece, the OCR software compares the bitmap image with known characters and converts what it recognizes into individual letters. It has more trouble with italics, bold, and small fonts than with regular fonts. It looks for patterns such as loops and curves to further distinguish letters it doesn't originally recognize. Whatever it doesn't recognize it replaces with a symbol, such as @, that can be found and replaced by a user reviewing the document. Users should review the document thoroughly for errors in the process.

Some software is ICR (intelligent character recognition)-capable. ICR software processes characters written by hand or characters in nonstandard fonts. It supplements OCR software. The error rate for ICR is generally high.

Considerations for purchasers of OCR and ICR software include the speed of processing and the associated error rate. Companies in the market for OCR software should test it by processing a sample of their own corporate documents. This step will determine a more accurate error rate for the system being considered.

A few OCR packages have reached the desktop and have almost reached desktop pricing. Caere's OmniPage Pro for Windows 95, at $499, and Xerox's TextBridge Pro 96, at $260, are the first two OCR packages designed for Windows 95.[12] "Lite" versions of OCR software often come bundled with the purchase of low-end scanner hardware.

Indexing

As part of the capture process, documents must be indexed. This process is similar to the manual process of creating and placing a label on a manila file folder. During scanning, a user may be asked to enter key words that will determine how the document can be retrieved.

The indexing function is automated in some scanning software. The software can get it from a certain place on the document, such as the top left corner; this can be programmed into the system during system setup. Or the software can be programmed to look for key account numbers, customer numbers, or special fields on the form.[13]

FIGURE 2.2: OMNIPAGE CAPTURES A DOCUMENT WITH TEXT AND IMAGES

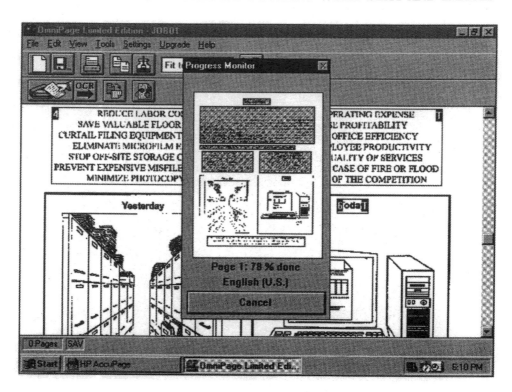

CPAs must put some thought into the organization and capabilities of the indexing function. Just as when planning a physical filing system, indexing will determine how documents can be retrieved.

The index file is generally stored in a separate physical place from the actual document files.

A Final Note on Document Capture

Good scanning techniques are learned. It takes working on thousands of documents for an employee to pick up tricks and subtle techniques that will lead to an error-free, high-quality process.

Document Storage

Several types of storage media are used in imaging systems, and each serves a different purpose. Before deciding on the type of storage medium to be used, a company should decide how long documents need to be stored and how often they will be retrieved.

The most common forms of storage media fall into two primary categories: optical and magnetic. Often a company will use both in designing an imaging system. There are several options within the two primary storage categories.

Optical

WORM is a high-capacity optical storage option. It is perfect for archiving data because it cannot be changed once recorded. Indexes for WORM systems often reside on magnetic media, so they can be updated often. WORM is the most common choice for imaging systems.

Magneto-optical storage is a high-capacity optical storage option that can be written to many times. It is useful for imaging systems that store documents that will be modified.

CD-ROM (compact disc-read only memory) technology allows a user to press information on a CD that cannot be modified. Most companies do not have the equipment to implement this option. Generally, a company will outsource the pressing of CD-ROMs.

CD-R technology allows a user to write information to CDs. The user needs a special CD writer that is desktop-affordable. Be warned that premastering your own CDs is a learned skill and not for the impatient. You can reduce the possibility of errors (there are no second chances and a beginner is likely to ruin lots of CDs at about $7 a pop) by correctly installing and configuring the hardware and software and following detailed directions about how best to record. One tip is to put the data on a separate hard drive before recording, for example.[14]

Optical tape is generally used as a backup medium for imaging systems.

COLD (computer output to laser disc) is used to image computer reports and forms. Instead of receiving a large, cumbersome printout, a networked user can view, search, print, or fax computer reports online. COLD replaces an older technology called COM (computer output to microfilm).

Optical storage is generally cheaper than magnetic storage.

Magnetic

A plain old computer hard disk qualifies as a magnetic medium used in imaging.

RAID (redundant arrays of inexpensive discs) is another magnetic option that is now feasible in larger-scale imaging operations.

DAT (digital audio tape) is used primarily as a backup medium for imaging systems.

Jukeboxes

Jukeboxes are devices that store and access a number of optical discs. Considerations for purchase of a jukebox for an imaging system include capacity, data transfer rate, and data exchange time.

Storage Issues

Two issues related to document storage should be considered in a company's long-term technology plan:

1. The technology is quickly changing in this area. A company does not want to get stuck with documents that cannot be read by current hardware. Companies can anticipate this obsolescence by planning to update their imaging system every three to seven years.

2. The life of optical media is shorter than that of microfilm.[15] A way around this is to plan to re-record the information periodically.

Document Retrieval

Text Retrieval

Document-retrieval capabilities vary among imaging systems, and there is a host of issues in this area. A document can be retrieved using the key words that were entered in the index. But what if you would like to search the *contents* of the document for key words? This type of retrieval is called text retrieval. Every word in the contents of the inventory of documents is searchable. Some systems use query language and advanced programming tools to carry out searches.

On a Windows 95 system, the **Find** command on the Start Menu provides a primitive example of index versus text-based retrieval. If you wish to find all files with file names that contain the name "Smith", you would enter *Smith* in the **Named:** box under the **Name & Location** tab of the **Find** window. The computer will return the names of all files with "Smith" in the file name.

Figure 2.3: Retrieve Lost Files with the Windows 95 Find Command

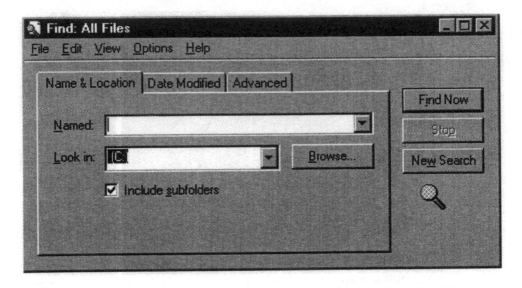

If you wish to find all documents that contained the word "Smith" in their contents, you can use the **Advanced** feature of the **Find** command. In the **Containing text:** box, enter "Smith".

A sample query took ten minutes to search through about eighteen thousand files on my local drive. It found not only my word processing

Figure 2.4: Retrieve File Content by Keyword Using Windows 95 Advanced Find Command

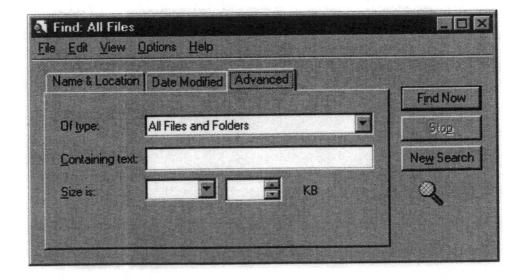

files containing this client name, but it also flagged my contact management software and my financial database as well as a database program I was writing for the client.

Some text retrieval systems search through only certain document types, so you will want to check the capabilities of the text retrieval software.

Version Control and Document Modification

A document management system should track who has a document "checked out," similar to a library card record. This is referred to as version control. Details such as check-out date and time, location and method of retrieval, when and how it was returned, and whether the document was changed should be recorded and tracked.

Document systems that allow modification to a document must keep a history of changes. A record of the original must be kept and changes must be "attached" to the original document. Changes can occur in a number of ways:

1. *Annotation.* Much like placing a sticky note on the document, an overlay object can be created to supplement the original document.

2. *Document combination.* A new document is copied from one or more originals. It has its own index and can be linked to the original.

3. *Raster editing.* A raster editor changes the image on a document and can create new images in the same way. The raster editor converts the image pixels (the tiny dots that make up an image; short for picture elements) into a bitmap (a type of graphics file format that can be displayed or printed).[16]

Backups and Retention Policies

A company must take very seriously the backup procedures it uses for its imaging system. As with any other data processing system, a foolproof backup procedure must be implemented.

How long should documents be stored? A routine for archiving older documents should reflect company policies and legal requirements. A purge routine to destroy older documents no longer required by the company should be put in place to further reduce storage costs.

Output

Documents that are retrieved are sent to the requesting station and can be viewed on-screen via a monitor or they can be printed. They can also be sent remotely, and fax machines are often used in this capacity.[17]

■ ■ ■

Audit and Legal Considerations

Audit Issues

Auditors involved with companies using imaging systems have some special considerations. Imaging systems often contain documents that support accounting transactions. Often these documents are copies and not the originals. The originals may no longer exist.

An auditor with previous EDP (electronic data processing) experience should have no trouble auditing a company with an imaging system. Audit tests on the conversion of documents entered into the imaging system and tests of controls will help to determine whether the auditor can obtain sufficient evidence to support a lower assessed level of control risk.

The designers of an imaging system must plan in the appropriate controls. Special consideration must be given to controls around certain critical procedures, such as document authenticity. When moving controls from a manual environment to an automated environment, there's generally a chance to improve upon the controls for that system.

A well-designed document-management system can enhance the efficiency of the audit by helping to document the business work flow and by providing a better audit trail than its paper-based counterparts. Computer-assisted audit techniques will further enhance the audit project.[18]

Legal Issues

Are optical records admissible in court? The following should not be intended as legal advice, and readers should retain their own legal counsel. But we'll make a few points anyway.

The United States and each state has a body of law called the Rules of Evidence. The specific rules vary by state, but in general they say that copies of documents are permissible if they can be proved to be authentic in content to the original. The Uniform Photographic Copies of Business and Public Records as Evidence Act reinforces the same, saying copies can be admitted as originals as long as there is no question about their authenticity.

Computerized records have been accepted in many court cases and are called data compilations or computer data compilations in legal terms. Courts generally have admitted other types of evidence based on the evidence's accuracy, reliability, and trustworthiness. Applying that to document storage, courts might favor storage media that cannot be erased or modified over storage media that can be. WORM storage, which cannot be changed, may have a slight edge over other storage options. This may account for some of WORM's popularity as a storage medium.

In general, the courts have looked to general business practices to determine what constitutes admissable evidence. If the business community accepts a document as valid, a court will generally follow that lead.[19]

■ ■ ■
FUTURE ISSUES AND TRENDS

We'll cover three trends emerging in the imaging industry, all basically good news for imaging users:

1. Increased integration
2. DVD (digital versatile disc)
3. Imaging on the Web

Increased Integration

1997 will see announcements of integrated products, such as the one earlier this year by software vendor Saros Corporation. Saros announced Discovery Suite, a suite of products encompassing imaging, document management, and work flow.[20] FileNet, the parent of Saros, is a market leader in this industry. It purchased several companies in 1996 with products that complemented its line of EDM systems.

Another vendor offering a suite of products is Optika Imaging Systems Inc., which offers File Power for imaging, work flow, and computer report management.[21]

Wang is also a large player in document-management products and, like FileNet, has been acquiring companies. Wang acquired Avail for its storage software, Groupe Bull for workflow products, and Sigma Imaging Systems for Windows NT imaging software.[22] Wang already has a reseller relationship with PC DOCS and Microsoft.

Products offering document-related functions, such as forms processing, will integrate with document-management software. For example, Cardiff Software, Inc. will link its Teleform forms processing software with Watermark Enterprise Series, which is produced by a FileNet company.[23]

DVD

First stone tablets, then paper, recently microfilm, and currently optical discs. One thing you can count on is change, and DVD will be the next generation of storage media. It is expected to replace both CD technology and VCR technology. Movies that cannot fit on today's CDs will easily slip onto DVDs, which are specified to hold up to 18 gigabytes.[24]

Imaging on the Web

Because the whole point of the Web is for people to view documents, it seems pretty natural to assume that the Web will be a perfect extension to imaging and document-management systems. Many companies think so, too, and are setting up Web-based document-management technology in their businesses.

American President Lines is one example. A large shipping company, it will make shipping documents available for its customers on the Web.[25] Banks are also allowing customers to view credit card receipts or canceled checks as part of electronic banking.

These applications allow viewing only, with no ability to modify the document. Companies are at work on creating the technology that will allow users to modify documents over the Web. Companies working on Web interfaces include FileNet's Watermark division, Wang, IBM, Diamond Head, and Siemens Nixdorf.[26]

■ ■ ■

SUMMARY

Image-processing systems are only the beginning. They provide a necessary foundation for other, more sophisticated systems. Once documents are digitized, stored and indexed, there are numerous possibilities.

1. *Work flow.* Document-management systems can be integrated with the rest of a company's systems through workflow software. This option will be more fully discussed in Technology 8.

2. *Traditional transaction processing.* Once accounting paperwork is digitized, accounting functions, from purchase-order-and-invoice matching to financial-report preparation and delivery, can become more automated.

3. *Knowledge systems.* Businesses have recently realized the value of employee knowledge and have tried to create systems to capture that knowledge. Document-management systems provide the foundation for those types of strategic systems, commonly referred to as knowledge systems. The search and retrieval functions in those systems can greatly enhance productivity and knowledge sharing. For example, if Don has a new client with overseas airplanes, Don can search the system to see who else may have clients with that same characteristic. If Don can find a match in, say, a client of Jim's, it will save Don from re-researching the tax and legal implications of overseas airplanes.

Image processing is the giant step toward the paperless office . . . and much more.

COMMUNICATIONS

TECHNOLOGIES

technology 3

A stand-alone PC today is as remote as an island without air service in the middle of the vast Pacific Ocean. But add a modem and some bandwidth to that lonely PC, and the world is at its keyboard. Connectivity is a key factor in leveraging corporate technology investments. This chapter will present the communications technologies that allow us to profit from this connectivity.

The first part of the chapter introduces connectivity options, from one end of the bandwidth ladder to the other end. The chapter begins at the beginning, with POTS (Plain Old Telephone Service), then discusses some newly available services: DSL (Digital Subscriber Lines), cable, and satellite services. The next section explores networking options, or how one PC can be connected to another. The options include network access, Internet access, and remote computing. The chapter concludes with four miscellaneous topics in communications technologies:

1. Video conferencing

2. Internet phones

3. Integrated messaging

4. Wireless technologies

■ ■ ■

BANDWIDTH OR BUST

Is ISDN (Integrated Services Digital Network) dead? Should we rush out to buy 56kbps (kilobits per second) modems? These are a few of the many connectivity questions being asked today. Bandwith is a major characteristic of connectivity and refers to the size of the "pipe" through which data travels. Most of the connectivity options, shown in table 3.1, can be used for Internet connections and remote network connections. However, some are network-related.

POTS (Plain Old Telephone Service)

Small businesses on tight budgets and home PC users rely on a regular voice telephone line when connecting to the outside world. The fastest analog modems for sale as of early 1997 were 33.6kbps modems. The actual speed of the connection varies, however, according to several factors:

1. Other traffic on the network
2. Noise and line interference
3. Amount of traffic congestion at the server
4. Server response

Because of these factors, an individual will rarely experience the *rated bandwidth* speeds that are commonly discussed. Actual speeds experienced when connecting via a 28.8kbps modem can be as low as 2kbps to 3kbps. However, because this relationship holds true for every connection option discussed in this section, we will continue to list the rated bandwidths of each option presented.

If you still have a 14.4kbps modem and you spend a lot of time online, it's probably time to upgrade. You are probably yawning between Web page downloads. As files get larger and as graphics explode on the Web, CPAs can expect response times from a few seconds to a few minutes to download pages and small files. How long does it take to download a file? The formula for computing the transfer time is—

TABLE 3.1: CONNECTIVITY OPTIONS

Option	What It Is	Uses
POTS	Connection via phone lines	Voice, Internet, remote computing
56kbps modems	Hardware	Internet, remote computing
ISDN	Connection via phone lines	Internet, remote computing
DSL	Connection via phone lines	Internet, remote computing
Cable	Connection via cable lines	Internet, remote computing
Satellite	Connection via phone lines and satellite technology	Internet
Frame relay	Data transmission protocol	Networking
Dedicated lines	Connection via phone lines	Internet, networking
ATM (Asynchronous Transfer Mode)	Data transmission protocol	Networking
Gigabit Ethernet	Data transmission protocol	Networking
FDDI (Fiber Distributed Data Interface)	Data transmission protocol	Networking

$$\frac{\text{Time in seconds}}{\text{to transmit the file}} = \frac{\text{Size in bytes of the file to be downloaded} \times 8}{\text{modem speed in bits per second}}$$

Using a 28.8kbps modem to download a 1MB file yields about four and a half minutes ($[1,000,000 \times 8]/28,800$). Changing the modem speed from rated speed to actual connection speed as discussed above will present a more realistic estimate of download times. Traffic tie-ups and server response are not factored into this equation.

56kbps Modems

Several companies are creating a 56kbps analog modem that will work over regular (POTS) phone lines. Unfortunately, two standards have emerged:

1. U. S. Robotics has developed a technology called x2. Hitachi Ltd. and Dell Computer Corporation are supporting the x2 protocol.

2. Rockwell Semiconductor Systems and Lucent Technologies, Inc. are proposing a standard called K56Flex. Companies supporting this protocol include Xircom, Inc., AST Computer Inc., Compaq Computer Corporation, Hewlett-Packard Company, and Toshiba Corporation.[1]

A uniform standard was expected to be completed in the summer of 1997. Vendors, however, did not wait for the issuance of a uniform standard and began shipping products in the first quarter of 1997, using one standard or the other.

Some users are troubled by the "double standards". Others are skeptical about the benefits of the faster modems. What will the quality of the connection be at the higher speed? If your connection is getting dropped a lot now, the chances of getting dropped more frequently could increase with the use of the faster modems.

Modem hardware is required at both your end and the connecting end in order to utilize the 56kbps modem technology. The ideal speed of 56kbps is gained only when the data is boosted from other digital lines, such as T1 or ISDN (both are explained later in this chapter). Two individuals transferring data between their two 56kbps modems will experience speeds up to 33.6kbps. Most analysts estimate that actual connection speeds will average about 40kbps.[2]

ISDN (Integrated Services Digital Network)

If POTS is plain old not fast enough, a CPA can move up the bandwidth ladder to ISDN (integrated services digital network). ISDN "takes the analog out of the POTS line" and offers a fully digital connection. Businesses with branch offices or home-based workers and small businesses with Internet access are driving the current demand for ISDN.

ISDN has been around for a few years and does not have a lily-white reputation. Problems with installation, ordering, and pricing are common. Users inquiring about ISDN in 1996 often got the runaround from phone companies: when the supposedly knowledgeable person was reached, he or she didn't seem to know much about the technology. Sometimes there is a several-week wait for ISDN installation; other times ISDN isn't available at all. Installation itself is difficult, and out-of-the-box solutions have not been developed. Pricing for similar services varies from cheap to expensive, depending on the city.

Two kinds of ISDN services are offered:

1. *BRI (basic rate ISDN)* provides both voice and data transmission in speeds up to 128kbps. You can split the lines and use one for voice and one for data traveling at 64kbps. But don't rely on ISDN as your only voice line into your

FIGURE 3.1: POTS VS. ISDN

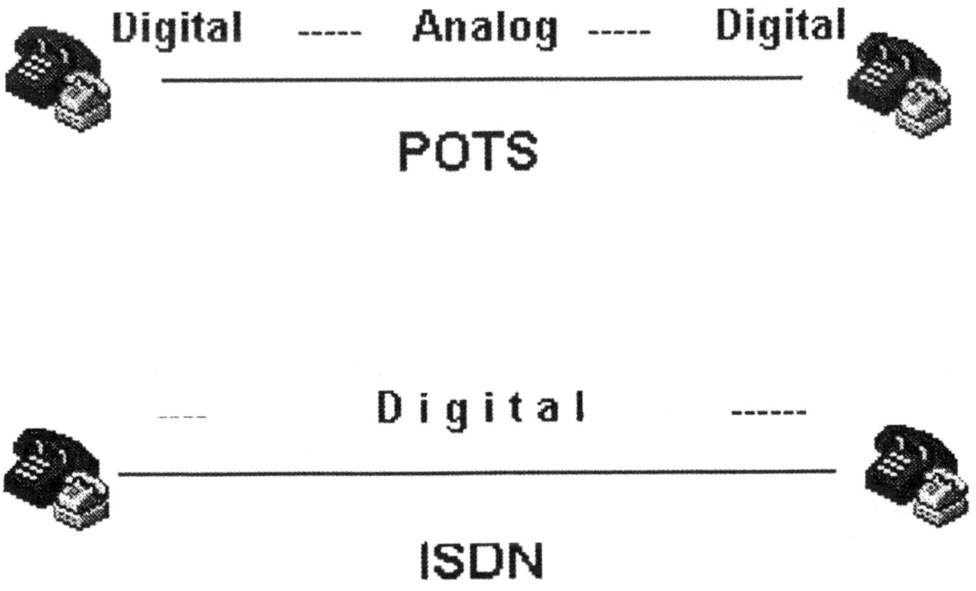

Digital ----- Analog ----- Digital

POTS

Digital

ISDN

business or home because if the power goes out, so does the ISDN phone. The best packages offer unlimited hours from $50 to $75 per month. Some packages charge by the hour. Setup will cost $100 to $250. Instead of a modem, you'll need a terminal adapter, which will cost about $200 to $400.[3]

2. *PRI (primary rate ISDN)* provides speeds up to 1.54Mbps (megabits per second), the same speed as a T1 line.

Be warned about billing differences between ISDN and analog calls. With ISDN—

1. Charges start from call initiation, not connection.

2. If you surf at the top speed of 128kbps, you are actually using two ISDN lines together. Staying on for fifty hours will be billed as one hundred hours if your plan is based on single-channel hours.[4]

DSL (Digital Subscriber Lines)

DSL (digital subscriber lines) is a new technology that uses existing copper phone wires and enables users to connect to the Internet even faster than at ISDN speeds. It was invented for video capabilities over phone networks, a concept that never caught on. Luckily, it is ideal for data-related services.[5] DSL will handle voice, data, video, text, and image transmissions. Carriers like it because it is easier to install than ISDN. DSL technology can be used for remote access to the Internet and to corporate networks.

There are several kinds of DSL:

1. *IDSL (Integrated Digital Subscriber Lines),* a hybrid of ISDN and DSL, offers speeds from 28.8kbps to 128kbps. IDSL is expected to be available in forty-five cities in early 1997.

2. *Symmetric DSL or DSL/384* runs up to 384kbps speeds. This version is effective for Internet viewing.[6]

3. *HDSL (high bit rate DSL)* provides up to 768kbps transmission speed.

4. *ADSL (asymmetrical DSL)* is available now in some areas. Asymmetrical refers to the fact that data can move faster downstream (receiving) than it can upstream (sending).

Initially, ADSL provides a downstream speed of 1.5Mbps and an upstream speed of 64kbps. Sometime in 1997 the speeds will increase to up to 6Mbps downstream and 640kbps upstream. Ameritech, GTE, US West, and Bell Atlantic were a few of the companies testing ADSL in early 1997.[7]

Of the DSL types, ADSL is receiving the most publicity. The asymmetric nature of ADSL currently limits its suitability for heavy two-way applications, such as video conferencing, but in the future ADSL will be useful for consumer applications, Internet access, or one-way video.

DSL technology will be available on a limited basis in 1997 as testing and trials continue to be performed by the major carriers. Most carriers are planning to roll out DSL more fully in 1998, and plan to sell DSL services from $40 to $100 per month, although the prices are not that low yet.[8]

Cable

Faster than either ISDN or DSL, cable, at transmission speeds of up to 30Mbps, seems a promising technology for the future. Cable lines are an alternative to regular telephone lines as a way for a home or business to gain Internet and company network access. More than 90 percent of homes are wired to receive cable (technically CATV, or community antenna television) over the coaxial (coax) cable network. A cable modem is required at both the receiving and the broadcast location.[9]

One big problem with cable is that the wide pipe of data goes only one way: downstream. To correct this, the cable infrastructure needs to be upgraded to allow two-way data transfer. Another big problem is the industry's lack of standards. But the cable-modem companies are not waiting around for these problems to be solved.

Earlier this year, LANcity of Andover, Massachusetts, was the cable-modem leader, with thirty-one thousand modems installed. LANcity's modems reach speeds of 10Mbps in a symmetrical architecture. Zenith produces a HomeWorks Elite product that transmits up to 4Mbps, also in a symmetrical fashion. If the cable lines have not been upgraded for two-way transmission, Zenith offers the HomeWorks in combination with analog and ISDN modems to handle the upstream data transfer. Motorola Multimedia's CyberSurfr receives data at 30.34Mbps and transmits up to 768kbps. It utilizes a hybrid fiber-coax network and a digital modulation

scheme similar to cellular-phone technology.[10] Motorola has received
1 million orders from cable companies for its modem.[11]

Cable modems will sell for as low as $200 in volume pricing (they
currently average $500), and cable access is expected to be offered at $30
to $50 per month.[12] Analysts are predicting that it will take about two to
three years before cable is widely available for those who wish to choose
this data transmission option.

Satellite

Access to the Internet via satellite is available now throughout the United
States. Hughes Network Systems offers DirecPC, a product that accesses
the Internet through regular phone lines as well as through a satellite
connection. DirecPC offers transmission speeds of up to 400kbps. It works
in conjunction with a PC and consists of an adapter card that is installed in
the computer, a satellite dish, and a cable to connect the two. The twenty-
four-inch satellite dish must be assembled and is installed outside. It must
be carefully aimed along a clear path to a specific satellite in the sky. The
adapter card fits in any open slot in the PC, and the cable is connected
from the PC to the dish.

To access the Internet with DirecPC, you connect via phone lines (either
POTS or ISDN) to the Internet service provider (ISP) of your choice. The
Internet data you request is sent to the satellite's IP (Internet Protocol)
address—by the telephone line—and the satellite forwards the data to your
PC.

The setup fees for DirecPC range from $700 to $900, and the monthly
fees range from $15.95 to $49.95. The monthly fees are charged by the
number of bytes downloaded instead of by the number of hours accessed.
The $15.95 fee includes 30MB per month, covering everything on the
Web pages and all file downloads. The $49.95 fee provides for unlimited
downloads during off hours, which are 6 P.M. to 6 A.M. These costs do
not include the ISP's monthly fee or the telephone line charges.[13]

Frame Relay

Frame relay is a packet-switching technology that enables data transmission
over networks. Speeds generally range from 56kbps to 1.544Mbps. Frame
relay handles "bursty" (sporadic) traffic best and will handle text and
graphics data. It was not designed to handle voice traffic but vendors have
compensated for this limitation by developing products that provide this

capability. Frame relay is a cost-effective alternative to dedicated lines (discussed in the next section).

By 1996, 15,400 companies were using frame relay. The revenue earned from frame-relay services is expected to grow impressively.[14]

Frame relay is most effective in connecting local area networks (LANs) that are separated geographically and networks that do not have a great deal of traffic. Its strongest benefit is its cost, which can be as much as 30 percent to 40 percent lower than that of dedicated lines. On the negative side, frame relay does not handle voice well and has a higher risk of losing data.[15] High-speed frame relay, at speeds of 3Mbps to 12Mbps, has just recently become available.[16]

Dedicated Lines

Dedicated lines are telephone lines that companies lease for their exclusive use. The only traffic allowed on a dedicated line is the traffic of the company that leases the line. Companies use dedicated lines for access between two locations, such as a regional office and headquarters. The price for dedicated lines is significantly higher than for regular phone lines. Dedicated lines are categorized by their bandwidth capabilities.

T1

A T1 line offers transmission speeds of 1.544Mbps. It can be divided into twenty-four lines. The cost of a T1 line varies by distance but averages around $1,000 per month.

FIGURE 3.2: EXPECTED FRAME-RELAY REVENUE

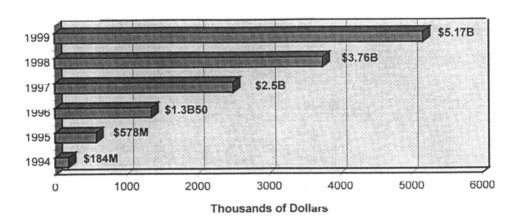

Thousands of Dollars

Fractional T1

If a company does not want to commit to a full T1 line, fractional T1 lines are available at half, one-third, or one-quarter of the throughput and cost of a regular T1.

T3

A T3 line supports a transmission speed of 44.736Mbps and is one of the fastest connectivity options. Also one of the most expensive, a T3 line costs around $10,000 per month.

High-Speed Protocols

ATM (Asynchronous Transfer Mode)

Initially, you might think of automated teller machines when presented with the abbreviation ATM, but to communications specialists ATM stands for *asynchronous transfer mode*. It's a packet-switching technology that enables high speeds of data transmission over LANs and WANs (wide area networks). (See Technology 9 for more information on LANs and WANs.) It performs at speeds of 45 Mbps and higher. ATM supports voice, data, and graphics; is good for multimedia applications; and is very expensive. About five hundred to one thousand large companies use ATM.[17]

Gigabit Ethernet

The draft standard for Gigabit Ethernet was due for completion early 1997, and the final standard is not due until 1998, so this technology is very new (Ethernet is a type of network card; see Technology 9 for more details). Gigabit Ethernet runs at 1Gbps, or one hundred times the Ethernet rate. Its simplicity is a benefit; its lack of quality of service, however, is a disadvantage as compared to ATM's quality. Some Gigabit Ethernet products will be available in 1997.[18]

FDDI (Fiber Distributed Data Interface)

FDDI (Fiber Distributed Data Interface) is an optical fiber technology that runs at 100Mbps and is very high priced.

■ ■ ■

NETWORK OPTIONS

Computers can be connected to each other in a number of different ways.

1. Through a network or a series of networks (LANs and WANs, to be discussed in Technology 9).

2. Through the Internet, which is, in effect, the mother of all networks (to be discussed in Technology 4).

3. Through a remote connection, as discussed in the next section.

Remote Computing

By 2000, 55 million of us are expected to telecommute, or work remotely, according to Gartner Group analyst John Girard.[19] Companies benefit from telecommuting because—

1. Communications improve.

2. Use of paper is greatly reduced.[20]

3. Office space and related expenses are reduced.

4. Employees are more productive.

5. Turnover and recruiting expenses are lower.[21]

What are the costs of telecommuting? The range of costs varies greatly, but the components remain basically the same for everyone:

1. Equipment is needed at the home or remote office. If the employee uses his or her own PC, the cost of this component could be $0. If a new, souped-up workstation is purchased, the cost could top $5,000.

2. Network costs include the cost of the lines and are the highest ongoing cost component of telecommuting, averaging $1,000 per user per year.

3. Equipment is needed at the "office" office and will vary depending on the network setup. The "office"-office equipment is usually the cheapest component of telecommuting.

4. Setup costs include configuring the remote connection which is often done by the telecommuter.

5. Support, training, and help desk costs are frequently overlooked, but make up a substantial percentage of the costs. If a user is undertrained in the technology, he or she remains a drain on corporate resources and is probably not reaching expected productivity levels.[22]

A study by Infonetics Research of 160 companies that practice telecommuting shows that most of them are probably exceeding their budgets with what they are calling "hidden user costs." These costs include problem solving—that is, the time it takes to get the technology to work instead of the time employees spend doing their jobs with the technology. A chart of the breakdown in costs is shown in figure 3.3.[23]

A company that properly trains information systems support staff and spends training time up front with telecommuters will have a higher chance of success with telecommuting.[24]

There are two primary ways to connect remotely: remote control and remote node.

Remote Control

With remote control, a person physically sitting at one PC can logically be sitting at another PC, whether that PC is across the room or across the country. Say you are at your office PC, but would like to install an updated spreadsheet on your client's PC about five miles away. Remote

FIGURE 3.3: REMOTE COSTS

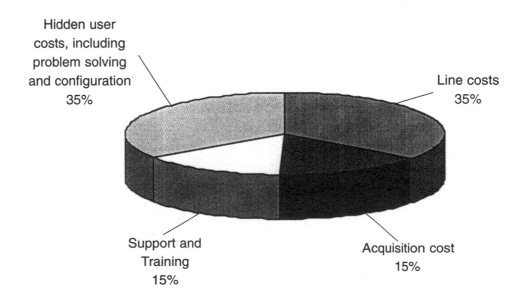

Hidden user costs, including problem solving and configuration 35%

Line costs 35%

Support and Training 15%

Acquisition cost 15%

control software will allow you to see the client's PC screen on your PC screen. The keystrokes and mouse commands that you make at your PC will be pulled through to the client's machine and will enable you to control the applications on the client's machine.

Remote control is most popularly used for file transfers between two PCs and for accessing files remotely. The remote user has access to all files and applications on the remote PC and can save work remotely as well. It is as if the remote user were right there at the remote PC. Remote control is also commonly used as an aid between help desk personnel and users who have a problem or a question.

Any number of connectivity options are available when using remote control: a cable between two computers, LAN or WAN access, Internet access, or dial-up via phone lines. Some of the remote control products available are—

- LapLink for Windows 95, version 7.5, by Traveling Software.
- pcAnywhere 32, version 7.5, by Symantec.
- Carbon Copy 3.0, by Microcom Systems.
- Remotely Possible/32, by Avalon Technology.
- ReachOut 6.0, by Stac Electronics.
- Remote Desktop 32, by McAfee Associates.
- Timbuktu Pro Windows 1.1, by Farallon Communications.[25]
- CoSession for Windows by Artisoft.
- Remote Office Gold by Stampede.[26]

In three separate articles, LapLink was rated highest for PCs running in a Windows 95 environment.[27,28,29] The product pcAnywhere enjoys wide usage by CPAs.

The remote control software must be loaded onto both PCs. To access the remote PC, the PC must be turned on and loaded with the remote control software. While the session is running, the remote PC cannot be used for anything else.

Remote Node

Remote node is the option of connecting to a network as if the PC being connected were another PC on the network, taking up a network node. The network must be set up for remote access, either with a dedicated remote access server, or with a remote access module on the primary server. The PC dials in to this server and connects as a node to the network.

Most companies are using ISDN or faster technologies to connect frequent users because regular phone line speeds of 28.8Kbps are painfully slow. The primary advantage to this method over remote control is that an additional PC does not have to be tied up. Communications software that is commonly customized must be loaded onto the remote computer. To reduce setup costs, training sessions for the telecommuter are advisable. Some larger companies even produce their own CD-ROMs for software distribution to a large number of remote users.

Roman Kepczyk, CPA, a principal and shareholder of Boomer Consulting in Manhattan, Kansas, lives in Tempe, Arizona, and is the quintessential CPA telecommuter. In 1996, he accessed the Manhattan office from Tempe with ReachOut remote control software. This year, he has been "promoted" from remote control to remote node. Using an ISDN line, Roman connects to the Manhattan server with Citrix Systems, Inc.'s WinFrame remote access software product. Roman says, "The Citrix box is a great solution for CPA firms. And by making the connection over the Internet, we save long distance."

■ ■ ■

MISCELLANEOUS COMMUNICATIONS TOPICS

Video Conferencing

If you can get used to a little jerkiness, video conferencing is desktop-affordable and a quick payback against those rising airline tickets. Sales are growing steadily. The expected growth is shown in table 3.2 as units shipped.[30]

TABLE 3.2: EXPECTED GROWTH IN VIDEO CONFERENCING UNITS SHIPPED, 1997–1998

	Business	*Home*
1994	30,000	0
1995	71,000	20,000
1996	200,000	100,000
1997	750,000	1.75 million
1998	1.75 million	3 million

Video conferencing has been used to speed product to market, bring team members together more frequently, and even diagnose illnesses more effectively.[31]

The market leader for video conferencing on the high end is PictureTel, Inc. Prices for products can range from $20,000 to $200,000 and are dropping. On the low end, Intel, FutureLabs, Inc., White Pine Software, Inc., InSoft, and Connectix, Inc. all have affordable products for small business.

A video conferencing system at the AICPA makes employees more productive. While still on maternity leave, a dedicated Nancy Cohen, Information Technology Section Technical Manager, joined in the August 1996 Information Technology Executive meeting held in Washington, DC.

Internet Phones

Software packages are available to allow a user to avoid long distance charges by placing a call over the Internet. Although very economical, these devices are not yet appropriate for business use because—

1. Quality is severely lacking—sometimes callers are not even audible.

2. The standard is just now emerging, and phones that do not follow the standard are not interoperable.

Currently, five hundred thousand people use the Internet phone regularly. As quality improves, this technology is expected to become a significant force. When will that be? When bandwidth increases, quality will improve. Also, when all vendors turn to the emerging standard, H.323, interoperability will improve. That's when you should buy an Internet phone.[32]

Integrated Messaging

With so many ways to get connected—for example, phone, email, fax, cellular phones, and beepers—we now need software to manage all of the connections. Not only that, but AT&T surveys tell us that 80 percent of the time calls do not reach their intended party.[33] Products that address these issues are now starting to appear. Wildfire Communications offers software that integrates calls, messages, and limited contact management in one service. To set it up, you train Wildfire to recognize your voice, plus you load your business contacts into its database. You can set up an itinerary to tell Wildfire where you are going, and your calls will follow, whether you are just in traffic or out of the country. The service averages about $150 to $200 per month.[34]

For small offices, a software package called FocalPoint by Global Village Communications offers integrated fax, email, voice mail, and Web access. A voice-capable fax/modem is the hardware required to take advantage of all of FocalPoint's features.[35]

A plethora of products is quickly being produced to forward messages and calls to multiple numbers, to read aloud email, to remind you of events, to forward faxes, and more.[36]

Wireless Technologies

The number of wireless products in use is expected to grow. The Yankee Group asked one hundred Fortune 1,000 companies what percentage of their workforce will be using wireless technologies. Their answers are shown in figure 3.4.[37]

A few executives are completely abandoning their offices for the road. Employees who are comfortable with technology and who should be in the customer's office more often than their own generally make good prospects for telecommuters. Companies with white-collar "road warriors" include Ernst & Young and IBM.[38]

Roman Kepczyk, our telecommuting-CPA-extraordinaire, says he couldn't live without his SkyTel Internet pager. "I can send and receive email on my hip." Now that's what I call convenient technology.

FIGURE 3.4: WIRELESS TECHNOLOGIES' EXPECTED GROWTH

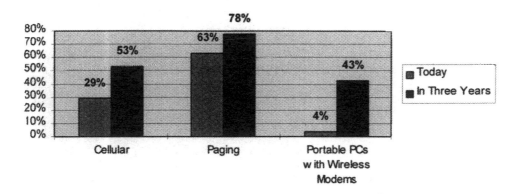

THE INTERNET AND

PUBLIC ONLINE SERVICES

technology **4**

On the phone with a friend one night, I was talking about shopping for a new car. My friend told me I should find out what the Bluebook figures are for my used car and for a new car. He got a long-distance call while we were still on the line and said he'd call me back. When he called back four minutes later, I read him the manufacturer's invoice price of the car I was interested in, along with the detailed equipment options. I'd obtained all of the information from the Internet.

I needed a tax form last year that even the local IRS office couldn't supply to small businesses and to those of us who do too few tax returns to subscribe to a forms service. The deadline for filing this form was fast approaching, and I still had no form. After trying the IRS field office several times, I located the form on the Internet and printed the form on my own printer. I wondered why I'd wasted so much time before trying the Internet. I was even tempted to mail a copy of the form to the IRS office.

The Richardson Public Library is only a twenty-minute drive from my house. Yet I didn't go there the last time I wrote a book, and I haven't gone there for this book either. In the twenty minutes that it would take to drive to Richardson, I can retrieve high-quality information from experts in Australia, Germany, and several states in this country without even leaving my chair. For that matter, I can go to Antarctica or Mongolia as well.

Much of my work is done completely online. Strategic plans, meeting minutes, and lots of business communications are written or reviewed online. These chapters are being sent via email to the AICPA in New York. No waiting for the mail. Sorry, Federal Express.

These stories are a tiny fraction of the successes I have had with the Internet and public online services. Jim Clark, chairman of Netscape Communications Corporation, has accolades for the Internet: "In the period of a year, Netscape [Navigator] achieved . . . twenty-five million users. That's never happened . . . in that short a period of time. The reason we were able to do it was because of the Internet . . . The notion of the Internet as a software distribution system is one of the root ideas to come out of the Internet."[1]

What can the Internet do for your company? This chapter shows you how to save time and money with the Internet and public online services. We'll answer the following questions:

1. What is the Internet?
2. How do I get connected to the online world?
3. Who accesses the Internet?
4. What can you do on the Internet?
5. What makes a good Web site?
6. How can you make money on the Internet?

The related topics of security and electronic commerce are covered in Technology 1 and Technology 7.

What is the Internet?

The Internet started as a government defense research project, the goal of which was to create a computer system that could not be destroyed by enemies. If the computer system did not have a center, then enemies could not destroy it, reasoned the researchers at DARPA (Defense Advanced Research Program Agency). The researchers created a network of computers that were connected in such a way that if any one or two were blown up, the other computers on the network would continue to function. Hence, ARPANET, the predecessor to the Internet, was born in the 1970s. In the 1980s, the National Science Foundation added a backbone network that linked many universities and supercomputing sites. Scientists and professors traded notes and knowledge using this network.

Private-company networks began connecting themselves to this backbone, and the modern-day Internet was born. Anyone with a computer, a modem, and an online account can access information from thousands of computer sites owned by businesses and individuals in two hundred countries. Although this statistic will be out of date when you read it, over 27 million people currently access this network.

How Do I Get Connected to the Online World?

Should you sign up with a public online service or an Internet Service Provider (ISP)? Well, it depends. With public online services, a customer receives access to not only the Internet, but also a community of other customers and information within the service. The four leaders in online services currently are America Online, CompuServe, Prodigy, and

Microsoft Network. We'll briefly discuss the top two, CompuServe and America Online.

We'll also discuss the option of connecting to the Internet via an ISP. Signing up with an ISP gives a customer access to the Internet community only. With this option, you would not have access to any of the online services (America Online, CompuServe, Prodigy or Microsoft Network). For example, you would not be able to access any of the CompuServe forums, where users leave messages and files about a particular subject.

Additionally, we'll briefly discuss pricing trends at the close of this section of the chapter.

CompuServe

CompuServe is the second-largest online provider with 5 million members in its community. It is best known for its extensive content. CPAs appreciate its business resources, news, and technology information. CompuServe forums are well respected as accurate, timely information

FIGURE 4.1: COMPUSERVE'S HOME PAGE, USING VERSION 3.0 OF ITS SOFTWARE

sources. In the extensive technology forums, sysops (systems operators) sponsored by CompuServe and the hardware and software companies help provide troubleshooting and training information for any problems posted. In the AICPA's (American Institute of CPA's) Accountants Forum, CPAs and other CompuServe members can trade messages about tax, technology, accounting, and several other pertinent topics.

America Online

With 7 million members, America Online (AOL) is the largest online. It is considered the most user-friendly and great for beginners and families. Its chat rooms are easy to use and fun to visit. Its user interface is full of high-quality graphics and is easily maneuverable. The problem of slow-loading graphics seems fixed in software version 3.0.

AOL has struggled with its fast growth, which gained notoriety during a 1996 nineteen-hour outage. Regarding that event, Mark Walsh, one of the AOL's executives quipped, "Our 2400-baud customers thought it was normal response time."[2] Recently, on one of my consulting sessions in

FIGURE 4.2: AMERICA ONLINE'S HOME PAGE

Dallas, my client experienced a busy signal many times before finally getting through. Phone line availability, modem speed, and number of phone lines will all greatly vary by region, so it's best to find out what a normal connection experience is like in your area before committing to a service.

Both CompuServe and America Online offer specials for new users that include ten to fifty hours free to try them out. Both offer Internet access, and parental controls are available for households with young children.

Internet Service Provider (ISP)

An account with an Internet Service Provider (ISP) provides direct access to the Internet with no access to any of the online communities. Heavy users, including researchers and technologists, will fare best with this type of connection. Users who plan to download many files from the Internet or receive many email file attachments will see a great improvement in speed when using an ISP instead of one of the online services.

Unlike an online service, which provides a seamless piece of software for Internet access, an ISP customer will probably learn and use several pieces of software. A browser, such as Netscape's Navigator or Microsoft's Internet Explorer, and an email package are essential. Other optional software packages include file transfer protocol (FTP) software, a news reader, gopher software, Internet Relay Chat, and Telnet. Recently, browsers have begun to add features for email and news groups, so the software required for a direct Internet connection is becoming more integrated.

New Pricing Schemes

All online services and service providers are struggling with the Internet's infrastructure. Some of the all-you-can-eat pricing offered by vendors has stretched the traffic limits of the network. Many vendors have abandoned this base pricing and are now offering new pricing schemes. Other vendors have abandoned the fickle home-user market and have focused instead on servicing corporate accounts. If you are responsible for budgeting for Internet access, you may want to account for a small increase in rates, just in case the trend in pricing changes continues.

FIGURE 4.3: SOFTWARE FOR AN ISP CONNECTION: A BROWSER, EMAIL, NEWS READER, FILE TRANSFER, GOPHER, AND INTERNET RELAY CHAT

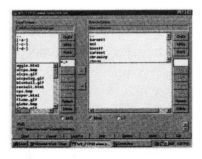

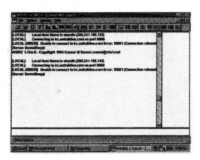

■ ■ ■

WHO ACCESSES THE INTERNET?

You can probably guess the typical online user profile. He is male, makes about $4,000 more than the annual average, and has more education than the average American. Women are gaining ground rapidly, but are still in the minority. A year earlier, the income of a Web surfer was much higher, but as more people have gone online, the average earnings of Internet users have decreased. Almost anyone in the technology business is online, although the Internet is no longer reserved only for geeks.[3]

How many CPAs are online? Well, the answer depends on whom you ask. CCH Inc.'s recent survey showed that roughly 31 percent of CPAs use the Internet for business. Whereas two studies reported by CCH, the first by *Accounting Today/Marketplace* found the answer to be closer to 42 percent and the second a *Practical Accountant* reader survey conducted in the spring of 1996 found 49 percent online. Of the number of CPAs online, 69 percent reach the Internet through one of the online services, such as America Online or CompuServe.[4]

What about CPAs' plans for 1997? From the survey results, CCH calculates that 60 percent of CPAs will be surfing this year.[5]

WHAT CAN YOU DO ON THE INTERNET?

What do people do on the Internet? A *Wall Street Journal* article listed the most common uses of the Internet, in order of popularity:

- Email
- Research
- News and Information
- Entertainment
- Education
- Chat lines and chat rooms[6]

Email

The number one application of the Internet is email. Over a billion messages were sent in 1995. Michael Kinsley, editor of *Slate,* remembers when faxes first came out. "Nineteen eighty-nine was the year you stopped asking people, 'Do you have a fax machine?' and started asking, 'What is your fax number?' 1990 was the year you started being annoyed, incredulous that anyone in the business would not have a fax number. Similarly, 1996 is the year you stopped asking people, 'Do you have email?' and started asking, 'What is your email address?' By the end of 1997 you will be indignant if anyone you're doing business with expects you to go to the trouble of communicating by less convenient methods."[7]

Recently I received an email from a friend in Kathmandu, Nepal. I had previously mailed him a magazine article I had written about my humanitarian work in his country. He couldn't afford to call me and,

FIGURE 4.4: AN EMAIL FROM RUSSIA TO DALLAS

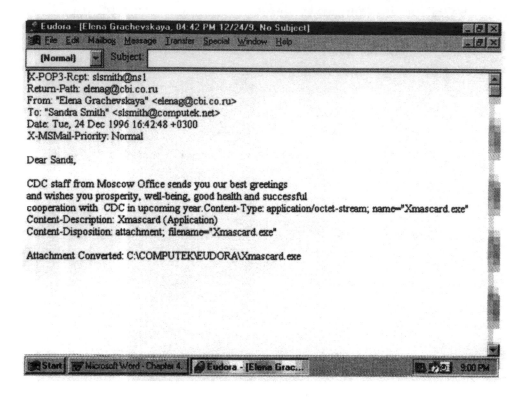

considering the time zone differences, probably wouldn't have been able to reach me.

Even if you're not from Nepal, email is a good deal. There is typically no long-distance charge and no delivery fee. If your postage or telephone expenses are over budget, email is a potential answer. An average email costs $0.02 per message, whereas a long distance fax costs $1.50.[8]

Email gives CPAs another way to reach their clients or employees. For savvy clients, CPAs can deliver at least some of their services online. Spreadsheets, engagement letters, newsletters, and even bills can be delivered via email, saving both parties the time and expense of delivering a document by mail or in person. Reduced travel time can turn into time for more billable hours per day for a CPA in practice.

Email provides employees at multiple locations a chance to keep in touch more often without running up the phone bill. Employees who are on the road frequently can also stay in touch with the home office through email.

Wouldn't it be nice if the phone hardly ever rang? That's the case at Microsoft, according to Michael Kinsley, editor of *Slate*. He estimates that 99 percent of internal communications arrive via email. And if you do get a phone call, you are usually warned of that fact via email.[9]

Research

The next most common use of the Internet is research.[10] Individuals can research a plethora of topics on the Internet, from job openings to competitive information, as well as Indonesian basket-weaving techniques and yak-butter recipes.

Technology

The prevailing topic on the Internet is, not surprisingly, technology. Many people use the Internet as a way to keep up with the maddening pace of technological developments.

■ **Topic Search.** A CPA looking for information about a particular topic on technology, such as image processing, can search for vendors on that topic, review products available, and then leave an email message for a sales representative to call back. In twenty minutes or less, a search on the Internet can give a CPA a pretty good start on almost any topic.

In the Accountants Forum on CompuServe, CPAs post messages about how they set up image processing in their firms.

■ **Free Software.** Free software and product demonstrations abound on the Internet. If you need to streamline a task, someone has probably already done it through software, and it is somewhere on the Internet. If you need a spreadsheet that does depreciation, don't build one from scratch; there are several models on the Internet to try. Shareware can be tried for free, but if you decide to use it, you must send money, generally a small fee, to the programmer. To give one example, I found two depreciation schedules on the Internet, priced at $25 and $30, a fraction of a CPA's hourly rate. How much time does your staff spend creating schedules from scratch when there might be something cheaper on the Internet?

■ **Troubleshooting.** Do your hardware and software hiccup occasionally? You can post the problem to one of CompuServe's outstanding technology forums and a sysop will usually answer your question. Need a patch or an updated driver? You can probably download it from the Internet, and avoid both long hours spent on the phone with a help desk technician and the wait for a fix to arrive in the mail. I have had excellent success with Hewlett-Packard's forum when I had trouble with a scanner, and Symantec's sysop bailed me out of a potential disaster with a client who was using Act, WordPerfect, and Windows 95.

■ *Technology News.* Sites such as C-Net (http://www.cnet.com), TechWeb (http://www.techweb.com), Computerworld (http://www.computerworld.com), and Datamation (http://www.datamation.com) provide timely articles on technology.

Business

The Internet is a gold-mine for business research. CPAs who wish to research businesses have several sources of information. One favorite is Hoover's Online, located at http://www.hoovers.com. A company directory is available for searching by company name. A listing yields sales and industry figures and a link to the company's Web site, if it has one.

Another favorite spot is the Web site of the Securities and Exchange Commission (SEC), at http://www.sec.gov. This site offers 10-Ks and other reports filed by public companies.

Jobs

Need a job? Or need an employee? Some of the best candidates now use the Internet as an additional tool in their job search. The Monster Board (http://www.monster.com) is one of hundreds of sites that post job openings for companies. Especially if you have a job opening that requires skills in technology, the Internet is a great place to look. The Big Six, state societies, Fortune 500 companies, and many more medium-sized firms post job openings regularly on their Web sites.

Cascade Technical Staffing places two to three temporary employees each month from job applications that arrive via the Web site. These applicants are more qualified than those obtained through want ads, resulting in much lower administrative costs to process the applications.[11]

You can receive electronic resumés via email or a Web site, or you can send the candidate a list of screening questions to be answered via email. You can even do a "phone screen" in a private chat room on America Online, although this is far from common.

Competitive Information

Want to find out what services CPAs are offering clients? How about what your competitor is selling widgets for? Companies that display Web pages on the Internet often display a great deal of information, including vision statements, services, industry experience, and prices. If they have a Web site, you can easily find out what your competitors are up to.

News/Information

Push Products

Earlier in 1997, "push" technology, which refers to how users receive information, was the hottest new item on the Web. Push products allow their users to receive predetermined information, making the Web act more like television as a medium.

The first generation of push software was called "offline browsers." To minimize hourly charges while online, offline browsers logged on, quickly grabbed email, stock quotes, and Web pages, then logged off. Offline, a

FIGURE 4.5: POINT CAST'S "PUSH" SOFTWARE

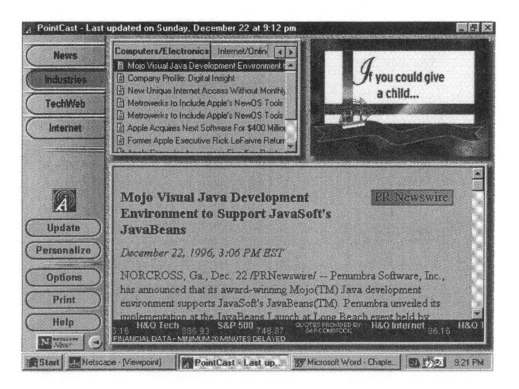

user can view the email and other information at his or her leisure without incurring large online fees.

Freeloader (http://www.freeloader.com), an example of push software, downloads several Web sites, then becomes a screen saver that switches from personal finance headlines to entertainment shorts. A user can click on a button to go to the "channel" in which he or she is most interested. My personal page in Freeloader showed the weather in Dallas, a link to the Fort Worth Star Telegram, and market quotes of stocks I own, twenty minutes delayed.

One of the most impressive push products today is PointCast (http://www.pointcast.com). Business articles, stock charts, and headline news can be customized to the user's selections and displayed on a menu. Update options allow users to click on demand or allow a stream when their PC is idle. PointCast software links with Netscape software to allow users to explore links from the downloaded information.

This year, Netscape is incorporating Castanet push software, made by Marimba, Inc. (the start-up run by Kim Polese, one of the Java creators), into its desktop software Constellation. Pointcast will be incorporated into Microsoft's Active Desktop, the next generation of its browser Internet Explorer.[12]

A disadvantage of push software is its increase in traffic loads over corporate networks. Some companies may find the increased demand for bandwidth a little too much.

A New Medium for Financial Information

CPAs provide opinions on financial information. How is this information being presented on the Web? Well, you may be surprised if you haven't looked lately. Many large businesses are using the Web to report financial information to the public. Here is a sampling of 1995 annual reports on the Web.

Intel has three versions of its financial reports for users, depending on their modem speed. We chose the top-of-the-line version, which uses Shockwave, a Netscape plug-in, and, although it took forever to load using my 28.8kbps modem, it was quite impressive when it finally arrived. A whirring ball grows large and hurls newspapers and chips through the virtual air. Click to see reports, footnotes, the auditor's opinion, stockholder news, or the latest stock quotes.

FIGURE 4.6: A SCREEN FROM INTEL'S ANNUAL REPORT, LOCATED ON ITS WEB SITE

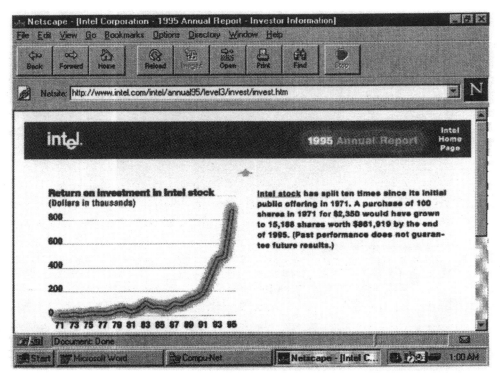

Both Microsoft and PepsiCo provide downloadable Excel spreadsheets with the financial reports in them, sans notes, that are fully editable. PepsiCo's income statement is shown in figure 4.7.

The Internet presents a great opportunity for businesses to expand and improve reporting of financial and other performance related information. It also creates opportunities and challenges for providers of assurance on such information.

Challenges include protecting preparers, assurers, and users from unintended association and reliance. Will a consumer understand what information is fairly presented? Where does the annual report start and stop? Will someone bother to read the notes to the financial statements when they are on a separate link?

The current auditing literature, including a recent interpretation (AU Section 9550, Interpretation of AU Sction 550, "Other Information in Documents containing Audited Financial Statements: Other Information in Electronic Sites Containing Audited Financial Statements"—published in

Figure 4.7: PepsiCo's Financial Statements From the Web, Downloaded Into a Microsoft Excel Spreadsheet

	1995 (52 Weeks)	1994 (53 Weeks)	1993 (52 Weeks)
Consolidated Statement of Income			
(in millions except per share amounts)			
PepsiCo, Inc. and Subsidiaries			
Fiscal Years ended December 30, 1995, December 31, 1994 and December 25, 1993			
Net Sales	$30,421	$28,472	$25,021
Costs and Expenses, net			
Cost of sales	14,886	13,715	11,946
Selling, general and administrative expenses	11,712	11,244	9,864
Amortization of intangible assets	316	312	304
Impairment of long-lived assets	520	-	-
Operating Profit	2,987	3,201	2,907

March, 1997, Journal of Accountancy), does not require auditors to read information contained in electronic sites, or to consider the consistency of other information in electronic sites with the original documents. However, the Auditing Standards Board recognizes the possibilities that financial reporting on the Internet creates and has established the *Electronic Dissemination of Audited Financial Information Task Force* to address issues raised by the above questions and more.

Additionally, the *Electronic Commerce Assurance Service Development Task Force* of the *AICPA Assurance Services Committee* is charged with developing an electronic commerce assurance service and to provide guidance for practitioners to deliver the service. As part of its charge, it is addressing electronic reporting on the different types of business information that might be made available on the Internet.

Entertainment

Many people use the Internet for fun. You can plan your next vacation, for example. Detailed maps help you track the local area and look for convenient lodging. Many hotel and airline reservations can be made online. Tourist bureaus from all over the world list sight-seeing opportunities and tours.

Recently I found a site called Firefly, at http://www.ffly.com. In the movie section, I was presented with twenty movies that I ranked according to how I liked or disliked them. Firefly then suggested five new movies that it thought I would like, based on my selections.

Firefly is an early generation of a type of software called "agents," which can "remember" personal things about users. Already agent software is available to find the best online CD-ROM prices and do other personal online tasks.

Education

The Internet experience itself is educational. One cannot help but improve his or her technological skills while online. If you are a regular Web user, you will run into many new situations requiring new technological skills.

Beyond that, a CPA can view local continuing professional education (CPE) classes in his or her area and order materials from the sponsoring state society or from the AICPA. At the Ohio Society of CPAs' Web site (http://www.ohioscpas.com), a CPA can search through the CPE catalog by city and topic to find CPE courses. Bisk Publishing Company, a CPE provider, offers product demo downloads at its Web site (http://www.bisk.com). A CPA can order CPE courses from the catalog at MicroMash's site (http://www.icslearn.com/learning/cpecat.htm). At the AICPA's Web Site (http://www.aicpa.org), a CPA can look through a list of CPE courses.

Chat Lines and Chat Rooms

America Online is the queen of chat on the Internet. Its chat rooms allow people from all over the world to meet each other virtually and have conversations. Private chat rooms are available for business or personal meetings when the host wishes to limit the participants.

Other sites periodically host celebrities of whom you can ask an online question.

FIGURE 4.8: SEARCH THROUGH THE OHIO SOCIETY OF CPAS' CPE
OFFERINGS

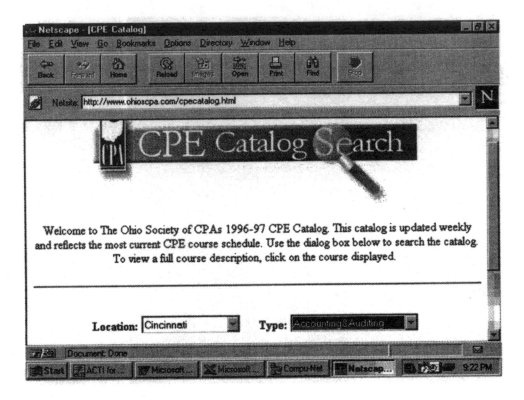

What Do CPAs Do on the Internet?

A survey of CPAs by CCH Inc. showed that CPAs use the Internet for
about the same things as the general public:

- Email
- Business research
- Download software
- Information transfer
- Accessing news groups
- Purchases[13]

FIGURE 4.9: A CHANCE TO CHAT WITH RITA COOLIDGE, SPONSORED BY
PEOPLE MAGAZINE

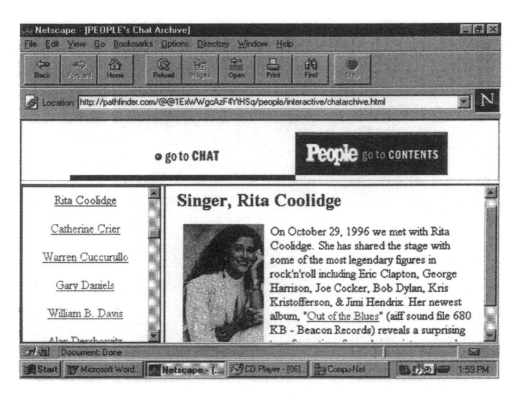

■■■

WHAT MAKES A GOOD WEB SITE?

Hundreds of CPAs already have Web sites, and thousands more are
considering them. What can a CPA do to get the most return from a Web
site?

More Than Brochures

Many companies' Web sites are simply online brochures. That's not
enough to attract the average Web surfer. So if that's all you plan to do,
you may be disappointed in the return on your investment.

Give Them Something Free

Internet users are accustomed to receiving something for nothing, and
successful sites play into this habit.

- At Ernst and Young, I found an Information Security Survey where I can check to see if my firm is following the top ten security tips.
- Thomas J. Hahn, CPA, CFP (htp://www.hahn-cpa.com), presents the Employee vs. Contractor Rules so I can see if my small business is at risk for payroll taxes.
- Groen, Kluka and Company, PC (http://www.gkcopc.com) helped me find out whether my company met the new limits on EFTPS (Electronic Federal Tax Payment System).

Each of these sites has given users enough information to answer their questions. If customers can rely on you to answer their questions, they'll call to inquire about your services. When you tell them you can solve all their small business needs, you have full-service clients for life. Well, potentially.

The Ernst & Young page additionally contains a button at the bottom that says "Click here to receive a full copy of the survey." This method allows Ernst & Young to subtly collect a browser's address. Now the prospect is on the mailing list, only moments away from being a new client. Well, potentially.

Ridout Plastics simply has forty to fifty pages of product information on the Web, which generate three to four leads per day. These leads translate into $5,000 to $7,000 worth of business per month, well above the $500 monthly cost of renting a Web server and maintaining the site.[14]

Boyd Coffee Company's Web site generates fifty to one hundred "serious" leads each month. It has fewer than ten Web pages about the products that it sells. When an inquiry is received via email, it is forwarded to a sales representative or entered into a system that tracks leads.[15]

Incorporate Multimedia and Interactivity

My favorite "sales" site to demonstrate interactivity is the BMW site (http://www.bmwusa.com). You can actually build your own Z3 Roadster and view the final product (and its price) online. The site involves the user as it presents options to select, such as heated seats and onboard computer. The user selects the paint color from a glossy selection of graphics that look just like those panels at the dealership. Select the interior and wait a few moments; high-quality graphics of your custom-built Z3 appear on the screen. Just below, click on a link for your nearest dealership.

FIGURE 4.10: BMW's BUILD YOUR OWN ROADSTER WEB PAGE

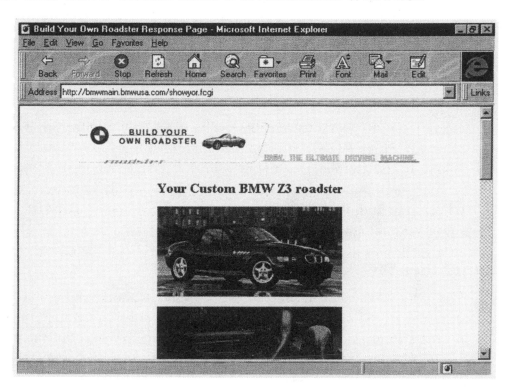

That's not all. You can download a three-dimensional file complete with the revving sound of the engine. The VRML (Virtual Reality Modeling Language) image can be whirled and rotated with a "push" (drag) of the mouse.

How can CPAs involve the consumer in their sites? Of course, the answer will depend on the CPA's business. A financial planner can help a user dream about debt reduction or retirement planning by having the user enter a few numbers and presenting some basic solutions. Graphics showing vacation homes or trips to exotic locations can entice the customer to think about his or her savings goals. At the bottom of the page, the CPA can provide an email address or a phone number that the customer can call for more information.

H&R Block provides a refund calculator. The customer types in information about income and deductions and the Web calculator will figure the approximate refund (http://www.hrblock.com/tax/refnd/). Deloitte & Touche offers tips about taxes and personal finances. They will send tax update news via email to subscribers (http://www.dtonline.com).[16]

CPAs in industry can use similar ideas to showcase their employer's products and services. Ask yourself, How can I involve the user at my Web site? How can I incorporate tasteful graphics so that my site (and my services) presents a competent, professional leading-edge look?

Use All the Senses

Don't forget to appeal to our sense of hearing. Even if your site does not have VRML or Java graphics bouncing around, it is easy to add a few talking heads. Customers who are willing to tape testimonials and partners who can espouse the benefits of their company greatly improve a site. Check out AudioNet's site (http://www.audionet.com) for the latest in sound technology on the Web.

Remember the Basics

I found a CPE course that I wanted to attend in another state, but I didn't have the phone number of the state society in order to register. I looked on the state society's Web site to find the phone number, but there was no phone number listed on any page of the site. The lesson here is this: Don't forget to list the basics, such as address, phone, fax, and email. Also remember that visitors from Denmark may be viewing your site, so include your area and country codes as well.

I Hardly Know You

Some users are put off by sites that ask them to register on the first screen. Don't ask for a user's address too early. Get them in the mood first: Give them some free information.

Yak, Yak, Yak

Another way to bring interactivity to your site is to allow users to post comments and view replies of others. One CPA answered browsers' tax questions on a *Washington Post* site.

Spread the Word

The potential for exposure is enormous on the Internet. Over 27 million people are looking for something interesting online. How do you get them to stumble onto your Web site?

1. List your site with as many *search engines* as you can think of. Search engines are Web sites that help you locate other Web sites. Individuals can enter a keyword, such as "CPA," on a search engine and receive a list of sites related to the key word. Common search engines include Yahoo, Alta Vista, Excite, and WebCrawler. There are some tricks to listing your site:
   — Some search engines use key words in the title tag of the HTML (Hyper Text Markup Language, the programming language of Web pages) to index your page; others use the entire content of your page. You'll want to use both the title tag and your page content to describe your services fully.
   — List *every* page on your site, not just your home page.
   — When you update your pages with significant content changes or add new pages, list the new or changed pages again. Some companies list their pages every month, whether or not the pages have changed.

2. Print your Web site on your business card and letterhead. Your Web and email addresses should appear next to your phone and fax numbers. You're giving clients yet another way to reach you, and they like the choice.

3. Link your page to others. Does your state society have a Web page? Ask them if you can link to them. Do you do business with bankers and lawyers? Ask them to provide a link to your Web site on their Web site. Just as they would give your name as a reference to a client looking for a CPA, a link provides a virtual reference and more exposure.

■ ■ ■
How Can You Make Money on the Internet?

There are so many ways a CPA can benefit from the Internet. Most CPAs I talked to feel that the information they receive from the Internet is its greatest benefit. The tax and technology information on the Compuserve Accountants Forum has increased his North Carolina's firm's competency and local credibility, says Gene Prescott, a frequent forum contributor.

Other CPAs find that email and information transfer are significant tools that save them time and money and increase their productivity.

Many CPAs agree that their Web sites or online presence via online forums do not generate a significant amount of leads or any measurable new business. But they remain sold on the Internet or the online service for several reasons:

- The wealth of information available, including the ability to learn from experts
- The customers' view that their CPA firm is a technology leader
- The prestige of being a part of the forum or news group and being an occasional contributor
- The convenience of email and file transfer for communication

A few CPAs are going a step further and offering Internet consulting services. Some of the potential services include—

- Web site design
- Web site storage, including renting Web server space
- Internet training
- Internet service providers

The best way to find out how you can benefit from the Internet is to sample its many offerings and see what works for you. Twenty-seven million others (and counting) have done the same.

TRAINING AND

TECHNOLOGICAL COMPETENCY

technology 5

"I had just gotten where I knew the Microsoft Office packages thoroughly," remarked Terri, a Dallas hands-on computer trainer. "I could answer any question a student asked. I had all the commands down cold. Then Microsoft came out with a new release and I had to start all over again."

How can a CPA afford to keep up with the changes in technology if trainers are having trouble? After all, a CPA might have tax laws, audit pronouncements, industry news, product and service changes, employment practices, legal and insurance issues, financial reporting trends, and SEC compliance to think about, to name a few. But the real question is: How can a CPA *not* afford to keep up with technology? Here's the answer:

Bob decided to upgrade his computer one day. When he did, his programs stopped working. He brought in a hardware expert who correctly upgraded the computer. This took a week. Bob's programs ran, but he didn't know how to get back to his data. He looked for a software expert. Meanwhile, a $100,000 deal slipped through his fingers. He couldn't get to his data to finish the proposal. Bob is now looking for a software consultant to help him get to his data.

Kirk spent $5,000 on a Web page. He hired someone to design it for him. The Web designers put a few pages out there. But no one can find Kirk's Web page because Kirk didn't know enough about the Web to know what he should get for his Web investment. He basically wasted his $5,000 because the Web designers did not list the pages with any search engines.

In Bob's case, he didn't know enough about technology to be able to get his everyday work done. In Kirk's case, he didn't know enough about technology to make and manage the right technology investment. Both of these costly errors are happening every day in hundreds of businesses throughout the country. Technological competence clearly affects the bottom line profits of businesses, including yours.

In an April 1995 survey conducted by the AICPA, CPAs were asked to rank the importance of trends to their profession over the next three to five years. The trend of "technology becoming a necessity in order to do business" came out on top, with 96 percent of the CPAs ranking it "important" and 58 percent ranking it very important.[1]

So what does a CPA need to know about technology? To help answer that question, the AICPA published a booklet entitled *Information Technology Competencies in the Accounting Profession* (referred to as *IT Competencies* in the rest of this chapter). It endorses and discusses

Figure 5.1: Technology Becoming a Necessity to Do Business

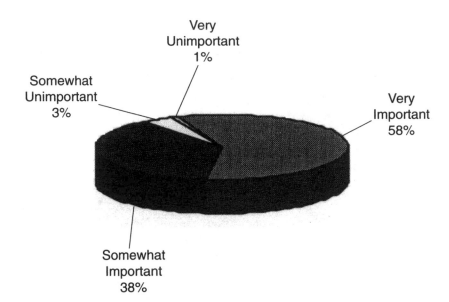

implementation ideas based on a set of technological competencies produced in the International Federation of Accountants' publication *Information Technology in the Accounting Curriculum.* We'll refer to the AICPA booklet extensively throughout this chapter in which we'll answer the following questions:[2]

    1. What does a CPA need to know about technology?

    2. What training options are available?

    3. How does a CPA get the most from training?

What Does a CPA Need to Know About Technology?

In breadth of subject matter, the field of technology can be likened to the field of medicine. Physicians spend years specializing in only one small area, such as pediatric neurology or invasive cardiology. Just as certain physicians specialize in these areas, technologists must specialize, too. Some become Webmasters, others project managers over accounting package conversions, and still others network administrators. No one person can know everything about every area. However, CPAs, like physicians, must gain a solid foundation of knowledge in technology. They must know a little about each area. They must know how to integrate and implement technology in their accounting and managerial duties. Then, they must pick up the specialty information necessary for their job or interests.

Because a CPA can be so many different things, what a CPA needs to know about technology will vary to some degree by what type of job the CPA is doing. The authors of *IT Competencies* present four domains affected by technological competencies:

1. Education, which affects accounting curricula at the university level

2. Work, encompassing public accounting, industry, and the public sector

3. CPE, involving continuing professional education course providers

4. Licensing and regulation, including state boards of accountancy and the Board of Examiners[3]

Leaders in technology in each of these domains will contribute in different ways to the profession's overall competence.

Education Domain

The education domain encompasses the academic community, which is responsible for preparing CPA-wannabees for their profession. It is critical to these individuals that the necessary education in technology is included within the curriculum required to earn an accounting degree. Two components are required for maximum success:

1. *Require several technology courses as part of accounting curriculum.* A partial list might look like the following:
   - General systems concepts, including types of systems, architectures, control, information, and related concepts
   - Courses to cover hardware, systems software, applications software, data organization, and system controls
   - Accounting systems and other business systems
   - Systems development and evaluation, as well as project management skills
   - Hands-on personal productivity tools such as spreadsheets, word processors, and databases[4]

2. *Integrate the use of technology into every accounting course.*[5] For example, in a tax course, the latest tax software should be integrated into lab assignments. In a cost accounting class,

one lab assignment could include determining how cost
accounting modules integrate with other accounting
modules, or evaluating several cost accounting systems based
on a company's processing requirements.

Brigham Young University has found success by integrating technological
topics with accounting courses in its accounting curriculum. Information
systems are the first foundation topic taught in the accounting curriculum.
Information systems concepts remain a central focus of the program and
are integrated with the accounting courses throughout the remainder of
the curriculum. In a survey of students completing this curriculum, the
students gave high ratings to their understanding of accounting systems and
concepts, as well as to the instructors who taught the integrated courses.[6]

What can a university do to improve its chance of developing a first-class
curriculum with the necessary technological components? It must ensure
that it has the backing of all the university leaders: the faculty, the dean of
the college, and the administration. The administration must provide the
budget for the training and the technological products necessary to support
such a curriculum. The faculty must quickly gain a mastery of each new
technological tool to present it in the classroom.[7]

A university must adapt its systems to respond more rapidly to the fast pace
of change in technology. For example, it must be able to retool its
curriculum to reflect the industry's movement from mainframe to network,
from network to client/server, and from client/server to intranet, all of
which has happened in the last decade.

A CPA candidate does not have to be a nerd, and it should not be the
intent of any program to impart engineering concepts or computer science
competence on a CPA candidate. *IT Competencies* suggests that curricula
using a "strategic" and "conceptual" approach be designed to teach topics
on technology.[8]

More than a few CPAs with degrees from the distant past are missing these
foundation skills in their repertoire of knowledge. Other than university
offerings, these courses are scarce and have not made their way into CPE
yet. And that leads us to the next domain, where most of us reside. How
can those of us who have already graduated get the technological skills that
we need?

Work Domain

IT Competencies prescribes four possible roles for CPAs wishing to learn about technology:

1. The role of the information technology user
2. The role of the information technology manager
3. The role of the information technology designer
4. The role of the information technology evaluator

These roles are presented *in addition to* the requirement of gaining a general foundation of knowledge that applies across all roles. CPAs will probably find themselves in at least two roles and should learn the corresponding subject matter in order to maximize their effectiveness with technology.

A CPA as an Information Technology User

To start with, a CPA can look around his or her work environment to see what technology topics might be relevant to the profession.

- Is there a PC on the desk? Ninety-eight percent of accountants use a computer at work, according to a 1995 survey.[9]
- Does the CPA know which tool to use for a particular task?
- Does the CPA know shortcuts and time-saving tips provided in the tools?
- If the CPA doesn't know the exact keystrokes needed for a particular command, can he or she figure it out?
- Can the CPA get work done productively on the PC?

As CPAs spend more of their workday completing work on a computer, it is crucial that they know basic desktop tools. An example of an *introductory* training curriculum for hands-on computer skills includes forty hours of the following topics:[10]

Windows/GUI (graphical user interface)	4 hours
Network Orientation and Online Services	4 hours
Spreadsheets	8 hours
Word Processing	8 hours
Database Basics	8 hours
Integrated Financial Reporting	8 hours

A good course will combine industry *concepts* about managing information with hands-on skills in specific software packages. A great course will tailor the lessons to the specific work environment and show the CPA how to generate work more productively. A quote from a training article in *Computerworld* describes the difference: " 'There are a lot of people out there, for instance, [who are] training people to use Lotus Notes,' says Elliott Masie, president of the Masie Center, a technology think tank in Saratoga Springs, N.Y. 'There's another breed that knows how to teach people to use Notes to do targeted selling or competitive analysis.' "[11]

Further curricula at the intermediate, advanced, and update levels should be tailored to individual CPAs. A few of the topics commonly included at these levels are:

- Intermediate spreadsheet.
- Accounting systems.
- Network management.
- Online and CD-ROM research.

What about a person who has delayed learning about technology until now? Individuals who have never touched a PC are faced with several learning curves at once. To become proficient in just one subject—personal productivity—they must grasp terminology, keyboarding, mouse dexterity, file management, and operating system maneuvers before they can think about getting their work accomplished. The International Federation of Accountants estimates that CPAs with no technological knowledge will need 360 hours of remedial training and work to catch up.[12] The longer these people wait, the worse it gets.

Where can you go if you have a question or two about technology in the normal course of your day? To enhance employees' productivity with technological tools, many companies provide a help desk function, or a place where employees can call with technology questions. Other companies provide a list of resident experts in certain tools that other employees can contact for questions. In either case, it makes good business sense to identify a contact who can answer technology questions. If an in-house expert is not available, a consultant can fill the role.

Companies should consider the costs of each of the above solutions before deciding on a particular course of action. If an accountant is interrupting a co-worker who has a $150-per-hour billing rate, it may be more cost-effective to hire a help desk technician at $50-per-hour to help that accountant.

A CPA as an Information Technology Manager

Thousands of CPAs act as chief information officers (CIOs). In this capacity, a CPA must understand the management side of technology. He or she must possess the skills to effectively allocate limited budget dollars to the best technologies and training programs, and must understand how to create and implement a technology plan for his or her organization or clients. A CPA must comprehend the strategic considerations as well as operational and administrative issues.

Some of the major managerial competencies listed in *IT Competencies* include—

- Strategic considerations in information technology development
- Administrative issues
- Financial control over information technology
- Operational issues
- Applications development management, which includes—
  — Systems acquisition, development and implementation
  — Systems maintenance and change
- Management of end–user computing[13]

One important component of managing systems is risk management, which includes disaster-recovery planning, security and controls, and identification and management of any breach of controls. This area deserves special attention because of its rapid, recent increase in complexity. The rise in remote users and increase in Internet access, for example, add complexity to a manager's job. The topic of security is covered more fully in Technology 1.

A CPA as an Information Technology Evaluator or Designer

CPAs who design systems, either for their own firm or for clients, must understand systems design concepts, systems project life cycle components, and systems acquisition methods.[14] CPAs who evaluate systems will need to know evaluation methods and how to implement them.[15]

The jobs of systems design and evaluation require a great deal of training and experience in the field of information technology. Professionals make wrong decisions every day, and occasionally the decisions are fatal to their firms. FoxMeyer Corporation, a fast-growing $5 billion drug distributor, decided to install a state-of-the-art, fully automated warehousing system.

By day three, the system had lost so many orders, overshipped products, and was such a disaster that FoxMeyer had to shut down. It later declared bankruptcy. FoxMeyer bet the company on the new system and lost.

Although the case of FoxMeyer is an extreme example, it points out that selecting systems is a challenging job that will affect the company's bottom line, positively or negatively. CPAs who have responsibility in this area will do best with a good foundation of education and experience in systems design and evaluation concepts and techniques.

CPE Domain

For those of us wishing to obtain training in technology that is customized to our profession, CPE seems like the best answer. However, technology CPE has a long way to go.

The fact is that technology CPE is hard to find in our profession. Why? Some of the reasons might be these:

- Many vendors are hesitant to offer classes different from their bread and butter lineup of accounting, auditing, and tax.
- Some CPE vendors and state societies set their schedule a year ahead of time. By the time the course is offered, it could be obsolete, or not as relevant as it was when the training calendar was set or the materials were written.
- Many CPAs do not know what they need and are not buying CPE courses, or they are using other avenues for learning about technology.

The CPE topics that seem to be most available include

- Training on desktop tools, such as spreadsheets and word processors.
- Training on the Internet, including email, research, and Web site design.
- Training on electronic data processing (EDP) auditing.

As you can see, this list does not scratch the surface of what a CPA needs to know about technology. CPE providers have three major jobs:

1. To provide more technological courses
2. To integrate topics on technology into current offerings, such as including a comparison of financial planning packages when presenting a financial planning course

3. To adjust their CPE delivery system so that new topics are added and offered quickly and material stays fresh and timely.

Until CPE providers and state societies offer the technology courses that CPAs need, CPAs can look for courses in the following places:

■ Technology training centers, including the ones at the computer superstores

■ University continuing-education classes and adult learning centers

■ Software vendors, for courses on particular software packages

■ Consultants who give one-one-one or corporate classes

Licensing and Regulation Domain

State boards of accountancy and the Board of Examiners are among others who fall into this category.

Most CPAs who are proficient in technology agree that there are not enough technology-related questions on the CPA exam. *IT Competencies* calls for reform of the CPA exam to ensure that new CPAs meet a minimum competency level in information technology.[16] Future CPA Examinations are scheduled to include an increasing number of questions involving technological knowledge.

State boards of accountancy are behind in their recognition of the importance of technology knowledge to the profession. The State of New York, for example, refuses CPE credit for all technology courses. Not only should technology CPE be recognized and encouraged by all states, but it should be counted as technical CPE.[17]

■ ■ ■

TRAINING OPTIONS FOR CPAS

How Much Time Do We Spend Learning About Technology?

According to a 1995 AICPA survey, CPAs spend very little time learning about technology. Most spend only one to five hours per month learning about technology, and most of that learning is informal.[18]

FIGURE 5.2: HOURS SPENT PER MONTH LEARNING ABOUT TECHNOLOGY

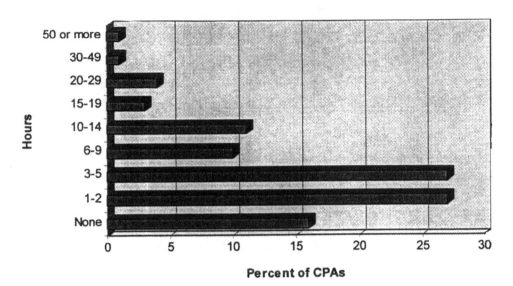

How Do We Like to Learn?

CPAs like to learn by themselves before they involve others or before they go to a class on technology, an AICPA Information Technology survey found. The top sources CPAs utilize for technology training include—

    1. Magazines and books (63 percent)

    2. Exploring new features on their computer (55 percent)

    3. Manuals (52 percent)

    4. Online help and tutorials (45 percent)

Getting help from others ranked fifth, sixth, and ninth as follows:

    5. Friends (30 percent)

    6. Staff (28 percent)

    9. Consultant (18 percent)

Formal training had a small following:

    7. Formal classroom training (21 percent)

    10. Conferences (11 percent)[19]

Another survey of PC users, not necessarily CPAs, had similar findings. This survey, more detailed in the type of learning activities addressed, showed the following ranking of the most popular learning activities:

1. Experimenting
2. Relying on program consistency
3. Asking co-workers for help
4. Searching program menus
5. Reading prompts and messages
6. Thinking about how similar programs work
7. Asking an instructor a question after a training course
8. Working one-on-one with a professional consultant
9. Looking up answers to questions in the program's reference manual
10. Asking a friend[20]

Reading magazines and books ranked sixteenth and thirteenth, respectively. Attending formal training ranked a dismal twenty-third.[21]

Although these may be the favorite methods of learning, are they the most efficient and effective methods? To answer that, we'll classify training options and discuss advantages and disadvantages of these methods.

What Are the Training Options?

Training can be classified into two very broad categories: (1) Instructor-led, classroom training and (2) self-study.

Instructor-Led Classroom Training

There are many variations on the instructor-led class. Among the more popular are the following:

■ *Hands-on Computer Training.* This class furnishes each participant with a PC during class time and allows them to enter commands at the direction of the instructor. Hands-on training is essential and effective if an individual wishes to learn spreadsheets or word processing in a classroom setting. Most vendors offering hands-on training keep class sizes smaller than twelve participants, so some time can be spent on personal questions.

■ *Satellite, or Remote, Training.* This allows a classroom environment in more than one location. The instructor might be in Seattle, while students look on via video-conference from Chicago, New York, and Dallas. A moderator is present at each site to administer the event and perform duties, such as funneling questions to the instructor. This method is cheaper than a regular instructor-led class because the ratio of students to instructors can be leveraged. Many courses offering this technology can invite national leaders and experts, and students benefit further from the knowledge and prestige of the speakers.

■ *Conferences and Seminars.* These are popular forms of classroom training. The lectures tend to be shorter and more numerous than in a traditional day-long classroom setting. Many conferences offer multiple tracks and a choice of sessions to the participants. Often, travel is required to attend conferences and is an added expense to the training costs.

The advantages of classroom training include the following:

- ■ It is effective for beginners who know nothing about the topic. Only an instructor can answer the type of questions that are asked in the very beginning stages of learning. Some participants feel a great deal of trepidation about the topic of technology, and some hand-holding on the instructor's part is status quo for many entry-level computer courses.
- ■ Participants can learn from and share with other class attendees. Some people simply like attending classes with other people.

The disadvantages of classroom training include these:

- ■ Classroom training tends to be one of the more expensive methods.
- ■ The skill sets of each participant in any one classroom tend to vary. The instructor must teach somewhere in the middle, with a risk of losing the extreme beginner or the intermediate user seeking to fill gaps in knowledge.

■ *One-on-One Training.* This blends consulting, coaching, and classroom methods to provide a unique alternative for some. The session is fully customized to the participant's needs. Someone who has gaps in knowledge but knows several basics about a particular topic will benefit best from this type of training. Also, those who pace faster or slower than participants in a traditional classroom environment will get the most out of this method of training.

Self-Study

For CPAs who are do-it-yourself types, *self-study* allows a formal approach to training in an informal, private setting. Self-study comes in the form of many media: books, manuals, videos, disks, and CBTs (computer-based training). The biggest benefit is that it can be done on the individual's schedule. It can be broken into as many time-segments as the user desires. The biggest drawback is that there is no one to answer questions. Individuals who usually pace faster or slower than a class and who can handle the autonomy and discipline required of a self-study course will find this method most effective.

Informal self-study is a large component of the broad category of self-study training. It includes many of our favorite ways to learn, including experimenting, relying on program consistency, and searching through menus and help screens. People who will benefit from this method tend to have a high understanding of the topic to begin with. They are past any initial learning curve and are successful at "snooping around" to learn even more.

How Can I Measure the Effectiveness of Training?

First, the true costs of training must be measured. Not only must the hard costs be counted, such as the registration or product fee and any travel expenses, but the soft costs, such as time away from work, must figure into the total cost of training. The time away from work can be computed by multiplying the hourly rate of the individual by the number of hours expended on training. It is the amount of unbillable time for CPAs in public practice or, for CPAs in industry, it is commonly called the amount of redirected effort that is unavailable for the current projects or regular duties.

When you include time in the cost component, an otherwise cheap alternative, such as reading magazines, may not really be cheap. For example, most CIOs I know read sixty to seventy periodicals a month to keep up. If CPAs read half that number, at forty-five minutes per magazine, they will spend twenty-two hours a month reading about technology. Multiply your own calculation by your hourly rate and add the cost of the periodicals to compute the total cost of using this training method. Based on the AICPA survey, this is the most common method CPAs use to learn about technology. But is this the most cost-effective method?

To measure the benefits of a class, a CPA normally completes an evaluation form at the end of class. This typically measures what the CPA *thinks* he or she learned during the course. But because it takes one to five hours of work practice to absorb each class hour of training,[22] a more accurate measure of the effectiveness of training would be to take additional evaluations in thirty and ninety days past the course date. These evaluations would not only measure course effectiveness, but also whether concepts have been applied and absorbed by the participant. Many factors enter into the success or failure of learning at this point. For example, what if the CPA were assigned new duties and has not applied the training? Only the CPA can determine the most effective methods for his or her individual learning preferences.

To find the most effective method, a CPA should ask:

- Which method will be most effective considering any special needs I have (such as being a beginner or having scheduling constraints)?

- How do I learn best? (If you have a preference and a proven track record, this method will take preference.)

- Which method will help me reach my learning objectives fastest?

- Which method will help me reach my learning objectives by spending the least amount of money, including the time component just described?

From the answers to these questions, a CPA should have a pretty good idea of the best training method for any particular circumstance.

■ ■ ■

How to Get the Most From Training

Here are miscellaneous tips to help you get the most out of training:

- If you attend classroom sessions, insist on shorter sessions instead of full-day classes. The absorption rate is higher, and our culture seems to be moving towards a shorter attention span as a whole. There's a label for this concept: it's called "Just Enough Training." Ernst & Young's training program emphasizes a hands-on approach and short "lecturettes" to "get [employees] going quickly."[23]

- Time the training so that you will use it immediately after returning from class. Again, this technique increases absorption. You guessed it: it's called "Just in Time Training."

- Training that can be customized is best. A trainer who can weave your corporate standards in with the training or who can answer specific questions will be talking the language of your work environment and of your employees.

- For beginner classes on plain vanilla topics like word processing tools, you may find some bargains outside the profession. Local community colleges and adult learning centers offer up to half off the going rate for similar CPE.

- For advanced technology courses, don't expect to find much inside the profession. Courses requiring certification, such as Microsoft's Solution Provider program or Novell's CNE (Certificate in Network Engineering), are popular. But these are not generally offered by CPE providers in our profession.

- If you have enough expertise in a particular topic, don't overlook the Internet as a great source for informal training. If you know enough to be able to sift through vendor hype and incorrect college term papers, the Internet is a fast, cheap alternative.

- Manage training as an integral part of your technology budget.
  - Budget $300 to $500 per person for training costs, not including the cost of lost billing time, says Gary Boomer, CEO of Boomer Consulting, Inc. and chairman of the Information Technology Executive Committee of the AICPA.
  - Evaluate employees' competency levels in the subjects necessary to do their jobs.
  - Create an individual training plan for each employee.
  - Select courses that are appropriate for each individual based on their plans.
  - Plan training into the schedule.
  - Support employees on training day by making sure their job duties are covered by a substitute.
  - Measure the effectiveness of the training on class day, thirty days later, and ninety days later.

> — Adjust the plan based on new competencies and training effectiveness.

- Trainers should be chosen and evaluated using the following criteria:
  - Knowledge of material
  - Previous business experience, including industry knowledge
  - Familiarity with business application behind training
  - Ability to customize training for company standards and industry examples
  - Ability to keep students interested
  - Ability to adapt training to learning styles and classroom environment
  - Availability on breaks and after class for specific questions[24]

- Training firms should be chosen and evaluated using the following criteria:
  - Quality of instructors
  - Reputation of firm
  - Availability of courses
  - Willingness to customize
  - System of effectiveness measurement
  - Extras, such as phone support for ninety days
  - Cost[25]

What Does the Future Hold?

Training in technology will itself continue to be delivered in new forms of technology. The Masie Center, a think tank for trainers, teaches trainers how to deliver training via desktop video conferencing, Web sites, email, and voice mail, among many other methods.[26]

Interactivity of self-study methods will improve with the new CD-I (compact disk–interactive) technology.

How Do CPAs Feel About the Level of Their Technological Competence?

The 1995 AICPA study asked CPAs to rate themselves on a scale from one to ten, ten being the highest level of technological competence, and one being the lowest level. The average rating was 5.7 out of the 10-point scale.[27]

On the same survey, most CPAs said they would spend more hours in the future learning about technology. How about you?

THE YEAR 2000

technology **6**

Going back to work is always a little rough after a holiday period, but the work week beginning Tuesday, January 4, 2000, may prove to be even more of a challenge for some people. Just imagine one possible scenario . . .

The power has been automatically cut off to about a quarter of the homes in your city. According to the utility company's computers, these homes, which all have their billing periods in the first week of the month, haven't paid their bills in ninety-nine years. Stumbling in the dark, you manage to wake up without an alarm clock. You think it's Tuesday morning. You're not really sure because your watch stopped working on Saturday (January 1). You drive to work with every red light flashing on your car dashboard even though you just had the ten-thousand-mile service done last week. When you get to work, several people are standing at the door. No one's entry card works. It appears they have all expired and the security system is locked up. A guard uses a key (remember those?), and you shuffle in with the rest of the employees. You get to your desk and notice your computer has taken a few liberties. It has completely emptied your email file. Twenty messages from the payroll system, dated August, March 5, 20;0 [this is not a typo] flashing in alternate shades of fuschia and chartreuse, require your immediate attention. No kidding!

Such will be the plight of companies that do not deal with the mother of all systems challenges, the year 2000 date conversion crisis. In this chapter, we'll explain the problem, discuss related business issues, and present solutions and tips for managing a year 2000 effort.

■ ■ ■

THE PROBLEM, EXPLAINED

Now take a trip *back* in time, to the 1960s and 1970s, when programmers began automating business functions such as accounting and order entry. The costs of storing data were astronomical in comparison with today's prices, and programmers were rewarded for saving space. A good programmer, therefore, saved money by storing the last two digits of the year and chucking the first two digits, which weren't needed in the calculations. Dates in these older programs looked like 12/31/99, for example, and translated to 12/31/1999. The day after 12/31/99 would be 1/1/00, translated to 1/1/1900. Uh oh.

Any program with date-checking logic and that economical two-digit year is a potential time bomb for businesses. How will the payroll periods roll

FIGURE 6.1: WHAT YEAR WILL IT BE ON YOUR COMPUTER WHEN THE CLOCK STRIKES MIDNIGHT, DECEMBER 31, 1999?

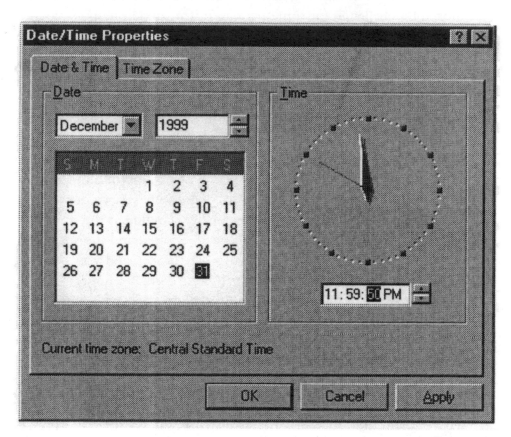

from the last week in 1999 to the first week in 2000? Will your payroll system write checks for people who haven't been born yet, according to the system? What will your aging-of-accounts-receivable program do at the end of January, 2000? Your accounts receivable balance might be a whopper with ninety-nine years of accrued interest receivable. What will your inventory quantities look like? Has the plant robot thrown out all of your product because the stale date has expired ninety-nine years earlier? All of the programs that do these functions must be identified and corrected well before the end of the decade. The jobs of inventorying, analyzing, correcting, testing, and implementing these program changes constitute a year 2000 project. And the problem is ubiquitous: few firms will escape the wrath of the century digit rollover.

In Denial

Are the executives at your firm savvy to the year 2000 problem? One executive who consulted with a CPA firm to correct his company's systems thought it was a virus that could be quickly eradicated using antivirus software. Others do not know the problem exists. Jeff Jinnett, an attorney experienced with year 2000 issues, quotes an Olsten study that shows one in six North American senior executives are not aware of the problem.[1]

Other companies that understand the problem may wait too long to do anything about it. Mr. Jinnett mentions a study by the Gartner Group that forecasts with a 70 percent probability that half of all businesses with this problem will not be able to correct it in time and will have at least part of their computer systems break down on the arrival of 2000.[2]

How Big Is It?

The simplicity of the explanation of the year 2000 date conversion problem can mask its complexity. The Gartner Group estimates that companies will spend hundreds of billions of dollars to fix wayward programs.[3] The problem shows up everywhere: in mainframe operating systems, legacy applications, minicomputers, client/server applications, and even PCs. A year 2000 problem can appear in a program written in any language: COBOL or C++, Pascal or PL/1, or any of a dozen other programming languages in which business and scientific applications are written.

Legacy Applications

A company that runs programs on a mainframe may have several systems, such as billing, ordering, and payroll, each containing hundreds of programs. Each of these programs could consist of thousands of lines of code. All of this code must be analyzed for any date routines that are contained in the program logic. Dates are peppered throughout input files, data screens, output files, reports, databases, control cards, and temporary working areas of programs.

In a program, all fields must have a name. A programmer analyzing a program for year 2000 compliance must look at all input and output fields to see which ones are dates. Some are named obviously, such as CURRENT-DATE, or MONTH-END-DATE. Others may be named whatever the programmer had on his or her mind at the time, such as a girlfriend's or boyfriend's name or code-like names, such as K7.[4] In addition to input and output, a COBOL program has an area called WORKING STORAGE. Temporary date fields can be contained here and must be ferreted out for analysis.

The programmers must trace how the dates flow through each of these fields. Sometimes the program is well documented because the original programmer described how each of these date fields was being used. Most of the time, especially in the older routines, there is no documentation to follow. Some programming code is so poorly structured that systems analysts refer to it as "spaghetti code". The programmer can use a logic tracer, which stops at each line of code to track how each date field is used in the program. Then the programmer can evaluate the changes in logic that must be written to make the program year-2000-compliant.

Not only must the program be changed, but there are numerous other components containing dates that must be changed. In a COBOL environment, a batch program is run using Job Control Language (JCL). If a file is expanded, statements in the JCL must be changed to reflect the new file size. In a database environment, components that describe the fields in the database must be corrected. In an online environment, the components that control the screen display must be altered.

If a file or database changes size as a result of expanding dates from two to four digits to include the century, data from the old format must be converted to the new format. A new conversion routine must be written to convert the data.

If the programs are very old (and perhaps the management in the systems department was not the best over the years), a company might not have all of the programming source code with which to analyze the programs. A company can continue to run a program with just the object code, a compiled version of the program, without having a written copy of the source code. In these cases (and there are more cases than companies are willing to admit to), a company has to recreate the source code, often by rewriting the program from scratch.

All of the above changes must be tested for every type of data the company might have. A company that has a good test routine implemented for ongoing systems changes will be more prepared in this area than a company with no testing plans or tools.

And, since all year 2000 changes should not be made all at once, a company will have to plan for bridge routines that will run in between the corrected applications and the ones that remain to be corrected.

The size of a company's year 2000 problem will generally increase with the size and age of the systems the company is running. With more lines of code to look through, the job will require more time and resources. With older systems, the documentation and code structure are usually poor and will take more time to review.

PCs

You can do a simple test on your PC to see if it will handle the year 2000 rollover. You may want to take a full backup before you start this test.

Set the clock on your PC to 11:59 p.m. on December 31, 1999. Then turn you computer off. Wait two minutes and turn the computer back on. What date does your computer think it is? Some computers display January 4, 1980. The results vary depending on how the BIOS (basic input-output system) of the PC handles date information.

If the date did not roll over properly, you can continue the test by trying to set the date (January 1, 2000) manually. After setting the date, some

FIGURE 6.2: TRY THE TEST ON YOUR PC

computers work fine. You'll just have to remember on January 1, 2000, to change the date. Other computers won't accept 2000 as a valid year. In these cases the vendor should be contacted for a BIOS patch. Other options include replacing the computer or using it to run applications that are not date-critical.

If the date is correctly displaying January 1, 2000, you can proceed to the next step of the test, which is to test each application that you run on the PC. For example, according to information at a U.S. government Web site (http://www.ssa.gov/year2000/y2klist.htm) Microsoft's Word 7.0 program is compliant.

The major PC vendors have begun to sell 2000-compliant PCs only in late 1996 and in 1997. Chances are excellent that most businesses will have problems with PCs made earlier than 1997 that are not replaced by 2000.

The State of Washington maintains a Web page that lists vendors and their responses to inquiries about their products being year-2000-compliant. Compaq describes the problem in detail and discusses how they have added a century byte to the CMOS (complementary metal–oxide semiconductor, a part of the computer that holds basic start-up information) to get around the problem in some of their models. Hewlett-Packard instructs users on how to correct their Vectra models. And Apple Computer announces that, since 1984, their computers have been capable of handling dates from 1920 to 2019 without failure.[5]

The Real Deadline: December 31, 1999, or Sooner?

What companies will have the luxury to wait until December 31, 1999, to put in their final fixes for 2000 compliance? Very few. Union Pacific began having year 2000 problems last year with a system that schedules railcars for five years ahead of time. After analyzing their code with Viasoft's Impact 2000, Union Pacific programmers found that 82.5 percent of their seven thousand COBOL programs totaling 12 million lines of code would be affected by year 2000. Their initial time estimate: one hundred staff years to fix the problem.[6]

Janice VandenBrink, senior vice president in charge of Visa's year 2000 project, started its redevelopment project in 1995. She expects to be finished with programming changes in 1998. Visa's systems must recognize cards with expiration dates several years in the future and must handle incoming transactions from twenty thousand member banks. Visa is finishing early to give itself a full year of experience with monthly and quarterly closings using the new program logic.[7]

If there are no earlier requirements, a company should plan to have all changes implemented by at least January 1, 1999, so that a full year of monthly and quarterly closings can be experienced using the new programming code.

Poor Planning or Millions Saved?

You might be asking how the systems developers could have made such a big mistake of leaving out the century on dates. Actually, it was on purpose, to save money. By leaving out those two positions for each date, many companies saved a significant amount of money in storage costs over the years. It seems a little silly to talk about storage costs today, when a megabyte of storage costs $1.08. But Leon Kappelman, an associate professor at the University of North Texas, has calculated some interesting statistics for an average company.

In 1983, one megabyte of storage was still a relative bargain at just under $22.00 (in 1995 dollars). But in 1972, one megabyte of mainframe storage was priced at $1,600.00 (in 1995 dollars). And in 1963, around the time when companies first began automating functions, one megabyte cost a whopping $10,600.00 (in 1995 dollars). So every byte of storage that could be saved meant big savings in systems costs.

Mr. Kappelman estimates that one percent more of disk storage would have been required if the century was stored along with the date. If a company saved one percent of storage costs each year since 1963, it has saved between $1.2 million and $2 million per gigabyte (in 1995 dollars, including the effects of inflation). If a company averages ten gigabytes in storage use over those thirty years, it has saved $12 million to $20 million. He goes on to add the effects of the cost of capital, assuming a 10 percent internal rate of return on capital, which brings the total savings for ten gigabytes over thirty years to a range of $160 million to $240 million.[8]

A company can apply these numbers against the year 2000 project cost estimate to determine how savvy its systems department managers were in those days. At the very least, a programmer worried about job security when notifying his or her management of its year 2000 problem can use the numbers as a last defense.

■ ■ ■
BUSINESS ISSUES

A brief list of legal, insurance, accounting, and general business issues will be presented in this section. The information in this section is intended to be general in nature and not a substitute for professional legal advice. Companies with year 2000 legal issues should consult with their attorneys.

Legal Issues

Legal issues abound concerning the 2000 date compliance issue. Capers Jones, chairman of Software Product Research, Inc. says that the average Fortune 500 company that fails to bring its systems into the year 2000 will cost shareholders $100 million in litigation.[9] A few of the issues include software-vendor responsibility and directors' and officers' responsibility.

Software-Vendor Responsibility

If a company runs and relies on systems that were originally purchased from a vendor, it should review any contract it has with the vendor. The company should most likely contact the vendor right away about the year 2000 issue. Some of the questions to ask include the following:

- Is the product currently supported by the vendor?
- Is the software year-2000-compliant?
- If not, is a year-2000-compliant product planned for a future release?

In an ideal world, the executives of both the vendor and the client will be able to agree on a solution that will work for both of them. But what if the vendor has gone out of business or no longer supports the product? What if the vendor refuses to change the product for year 2000 compliance? The company that relies on the software must look for remedies in the contract and seek professional advice.

Jeff Jinnett includes a sticky example in his paper at Peter de Jager's Year 2000 Web site. A vendor promises to deliver a software update in mid-1999 that is year-2000-compliant. A licensee of the software does not think the vendor will make the deadline and decides to reverse-engineer the code and fix the code itself. The licensee may be violating copyright law even though the deadline may be missed. Both companies have breached the contract. What are the risks of each company and how can they be reduced? These issues are best handled by professional legal counsel.[10]

According to Mr. Jinnett, any *new* contract to purchase packaged software should include language to "warrant" and "represent" that the software will be year-2000-compliant.[11]

Companies that outsource their systems functions must look to the outsourcing vendor and the related contract to determine the course of action that must be taken to ensure any year 2000 work is completed in time.

Directors' and Officers' Responsibility

Directors and officers of a company have a responsibility to make decisions in the best interest of the company. If the year 2000 problem is ignored, the directors and officers of the company could be considered negligent in their duties.

Company leaders should take care to document the steps they take in planning and addressing this problem. If a company should fail to become year-2000-compliant in time, this documentation could show that management was diligent in its pursuit of a solution to the problem, even though the deadline was missed.[12]

Insurance Issues

Insurance policies that could be affected by year 2000 non-compliance could include business interruption insurance and directors' and officers' liability insurance. Insurance companies issuing business interruption insurance may add a rider to specifically exclude coverage of a year 2000 disaster.

A company carrying directors' and officers' liability insurance may wish to review its policy carefully as year 2000 approaches. Companies with year 2000 exposure may be subject to additional disclosure on insurance renewal applications. Companies with year 2000 exposure that plan to change policies for directors' and officers' liability in the next three years may find themselves completing a rather comprehensive application when applying for new insurance.[13]

Accounting Issues

The Emerging Issues Task Force (EITF) of the Financial Accounting Standards Board (FASB) discussed the year 2000 issue at its July 1996 meeting. The members agreed that costs incurred in implementing systems corrections specifically related to the year 2000 should be deducted in the period incurred rather than capitalized (EITF Issue 96-14). The committee did not address new software purchased to replace code that is not corrected for the year 2000.

As the year 2000 itself gets closer, reporting issues will become more prominent. A company that is on track with its year 2000 solution will not present any special issues. But what if the company has estimated the year 2000 project at $30 million and hasn't started as of 1999? What disclosure requirements will a public company have in relation to this project estimate? There is nothing in the accounting literature that requires a company to report future costs specifically associated with modifying internal-use software. However, the SEC (Securities and Exchange Commission) does require a discussion of forward-looking data in Management's Discussion and Analysis (MD&A) and, depending on the magnitude of the cost, a discussion of year 2000 project costs could be required.

A company that is ignoring the problem presents a larger challenge to auditors. Should an auditor ask to see a company's year 2000 plan? Should an auditor qualify his or her opinion when confronted with a company that is not only running systems on old hardware that cannot be made year-2000-compliant, but that also does not have a plan? When does the issue become a going-concern issue? If the fix will take three more years and it is already 1998, is this a going-concern issue? Although the Audit Issues Task Force of the Auditing Standards Board (ASB) discussed the issue, they reached no specific conclusions, but noted that the problem did not impose any additional responsibilities for auditors. Auditing Standards Board Chair Edmund R. Noonan said a factor in the task force's discussion was the entity-specific nature of the problem: different companies will face widely divergent circumstances and therefore different ways for addressing the problem, so a generic solution is not practical. Because there are no specific guidelines on year 2000, the existing standards must be applied to answer these questions.

The best approach is, of course, prevention. CPAs who advise companies might ask management about their year 2000 plans and activities to ensure the company will become compliant in time. CPAs who suspect that management is not aware of the potential size of the problem can take a leadership position in educating senior executives on the issue. The

AICPA, in a joint project with the Canadian Institute of Chartered Accountants, is developing guidance for the profession on this issue.

Because this topic is quickly emerging, the reader is encouraged to check the recent press for new rulings by the SEC, the ASB, or any of the other relevant standards-making bodies.

Business Issues

Expensive Project Resources

Companies that procrastinate in correcting their systems for the year 2000 may find their project estimates to be insufficient. As 2000 approaches, programming and consulting resources will be overbooked by companies scrambling to fix their systems. Hourly rates for COBOL programmers were already rising rapidly in 1996 after experiencing a decline in the early 1990s when client/server and object-oriented languages became popular. Toward the end of this decade, COBOL programmers will become very scarce and very expensive as companies search for talent to correct older programs.

A Project That Cannot Possibly Be Late

There is nothing more challenging than a systems project for which the due date can't possibly slip. Even IBM and Microsoft cannot do anything to delay the time continuum. With industry statistics showing that only 16 percent of systems projects are finished on time, within budget, and with the originally planned functions and features,[14] it will become critical to use the best project managers that a company can find and afford.

■ ■ ■

THE SOLUTION

The steps involved in a year 2000 project include—

- Taking an inventory of all hardware and software.
- Contacting the vendors and reviewing contract agreements.
- Creating a game plan that includes:
    - An assessment of tools available on the market.
    - Decisions to correct, eliminate, or replace each system.
    - Decisions about how to correct the code by data expansion, logic changes, or a hybrid approach.

> — Policy decisions for year 2000 compliance on new items and contracts.
> — Budget and project approval.
>
> ■ Implementing the plan, which includes the traditional coding, testing, conversion, documentation, and training steps.

Take an Inventory

Start by taking an inventory of your computer systems. This can be a formidable task in itself. List every system, including hardware platforms, operating and systems software, and business applications. No platform is exempt: mainframes, minis, and PCs must all be included. Remember to list external interfaces too, including interfaces with customers and suppliers.

The inventory constitutes the possible scope of the project. As a side benefit, consider documenting the inventory in such a way that the documentation will be beneficial and usable on future projects. For each system, the original source of the system should be listed. For example, if a system was purchased from a software package vendor, the vendor's name should be added to the inventory. If programs were custom-written by a company's systems department, that should be noted in the inventory.

Vendor Commitments

For each inventory item that was purchased from a vendor, a company will want to find out whether the vendor will make the year 2000 changes to the product and provide them to the company.

First you may have to find the vendor. Tracking a vendor that is out of business or has been acquired by another company may take a bit of sleuthing. Once you find the vendor, ask what the vendor intends to do about the product. Is it already year-2000-compliant? Will it be in the next release? Is that release in your budget and time schedule? These negotiations should be conducted at the executive level by both companies. Information technologist Carl Roecker says Texaco learned not to waste time having lower-level staff conduct these conversations.[15]

Three Web sites that contain information about vendor compliance are—

1. The State of Washington, at http://www.wa.gov/dis/2000/y2000.htm. This site includes responses from vendors.

2. The General Services Administration (GSA), at htttp://www.ssa.gov/year2000/y2klist.htm. This site lists hundreds of products, often by release number, and whether they are compliant according to government studies.

3. IBM's site at http://www.s390.ibm.com/stories/tran2000.htm, which includes a downloadable document about IBM products.

Tools

More than forty vendors have responded to the year 2000 crisis with products to ease a company through its project. The products vary from estimating and inventorying tools to date routines and code analyzers. The vendors include Computer Associates, CompuWare, Micro Focus Inc. and Viasoft. Three Web sites are useful in finding out about these tools, as well

FIGURE 6.3: THE STATE OF WASHINGTON'S YEAR 2000 WEB PAGE

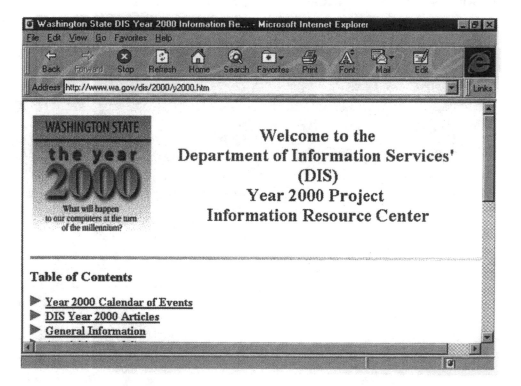

as additional vendors and consultants that provide tools and services to address year 2000 projects:

1. Peter de Jager's Web site at http://www.year2000.com has a list of vendors that provide year 2000 products and services.

2. An article about a few of the year 2000 products is listed at http://techweb.cmp.com/iw/565/65olyr2.htm.

3. Auditserve, Inc. provides a four-hundred-page book on the year 2000 with a comprehensive listing of vendors and products at http://www.auditserve.com/. (Be warned the book costs $995.00.)

Tools that can be useful for future systems enhancements will help a company gain the most out of its year 2000 expenditures.

Replace, Can, or Fix

Which systems will still be running in 2000 and which systems will definitely be replaced before 2000? Obviously you won't need to fix the

FIGURE 6.4: PETER DE JAGER'S YEAR 2000 WEB SITE

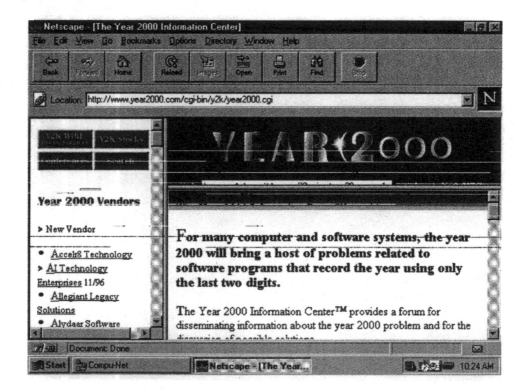

systems you will be replacing, but you will need enough systems staff to handle all of the projects that you are planning in this time frame.

You have another option as well, and that is to eliminate the system. Once, as a part of a Fortune 500 systems department, my team decided to stop producing some older reports to see if anyone missed them. No one did. Some systems may be so old that no one remembers what they do or no one cares. In some companies, pulling the plug on a long-forgotten system will be a cost-effective option.

To finalize this step, note on the inventory the action to be taken with each system: replace, eliminate, or fix.

Three Approaches

A company may take one of three approaches in solving the year 2000 problem.

1. It can add the century to every date field in its systems.

2. It can change the programming logic to determine the correct year without expanding the date fields in files.

3. It can also produce a hybrid solution, using either of the first two approaches in certain cases.

To add the century to every date field, a company will simply expand all date fields from two digits to four digits. It must subsequently test the program logic to ensure compliance with the expanded date. This solution is the best long-term answer for a company.

Changing the programming logic without expanding the date fields in files is another solution. I first corrected a noncompliant code using this method in 1983. The logic in a COBOL problem (presented in English) would look like this:

> →If the value of a date is less than 80 (meaning the year is earlier than 1980)
>> Make the century value 2000
> →Otherwise (the date must be later than 1980)
>> Make the century value 1900

The century value is temporarily stored in memory but never added to the files. This logic will not work correctly for years earlier than 1980 or later than 2079. But if for some reason the files cannot be expanded, this method is an option.

Policy Prevention for the Future

Immediately a company should begin buying year-2000-compliant products only. If it doesn't, the problem will only get larger. Companies entering into contracts with software and hardware vendors should include a year 2000 clause in their contracts. Wording for this clause is widely available on the Internet, although your company attorney should be the final authority on all corporate contracts.

Budget and Approval

Once a strategy for each system is determined, a project budget can be estimated. The Gartner Group, Inc. estimates that companies using the logic method to fix the year 2000 problem will spend $1.10 per line of COBOL code. The data expansion method is more expensive, at $1.65 per line of COBOL code.[16] The Department of Defense, which has 358 million lines of code, estimates its 2000 costs will range from $1.02 to $8.52 per line of code.[17]

Getting the money for a year 2000 project is a significant hurdle in some companies. One programmer commented that he "raised the red flag" on the year 2000 issue in 1994 and was laughed out of the executive suite. If executives are balking at the project or the money, project managers must resort to "get tough" tactics:

- Show exactly which systems will fail and list the potential for lost revenue and increased costs.
- Describe the legal risks, such as shareholder lawsuits.
- Provide statistics and costs from business journals, the Internet, and other companies that are facing the problem.
- Bring in consultants and industry experts to demonstrate the seriousness of the problem.[18]

Once a project is approved, executive support is crucial throughout each phase. A year 2000 project manager should have enough power to cut through any political issues that develop that could slow down the project. One consultant recommends having the year 2000 project manager report directly to the president of the organization.[19]

Tips on stretching the year 2000 budget:

- Start early. If your company needs outside resources to complete the project, they will become more scarce and more expensive the longer a company waits. Salaries for year 2000 project managers are already six figures a year.

- Document and maintain your inventory of hardware, systems, and programs so that it can be used in future enhancement projects.

- Buy tools that can be used to trace program logic for the year 2000 and that can be used to save time on future enhancement projects.

- If your company has been wanting a systems function that requires a change in a majority of its programs, include the change in the year 2000 project. Biamax SA, a Greek vehicle dealer, incorporated the feature of handling multiple companies in its systems at the same time that they fixed the year 2000 code. A forward-thinking company, Biamax finished its year 2000 changes in 1996.[20]

Implementation

The implementation phase of a year 2000 project can be treated similarly to any traditional systems project. Here are a few tips to get the most out of a year 2000 project:

- Plan to implement the changes in phases. Putting all of the code changes in at once could be fatal. Programmers can build temporary bridges between the old and the new implementations.

- Companies that already have thorough test plans for their systems will be ahead of the year 2000 game. A company should have a permanent, separate test system for use by the year 2000 team, complete with copies of production programs and databases.

- For systems that will be fixed using a logic-based approach: if a program has to be changed for another reason, slip year 2000 changes in at that time. Even if you haven't started your year 2000 project yet, you can begin to make changes to programs that are planned to be "opened up" for other reasons. A company that started this in 1985 will not have such a large problem as other companies.

- Understand the time each phase will take. Janice VandenBrink, senior vice president of Visa's year 2000 project, breaks down her company's project time as follows:
  - 40 percent documenting programs and designing the solution
  - 50 percent testing
  - only 10 percent changing the code[21]

■ ■ ■

How Is Everyone Else Doing?

You may not want to get a job being a federal information systems manager any time soon. The government is not exactly prepared for the year 2000. From a congressional hearing in April 1996, the first on the year 2000 problem, the government could miscalculate benefits, erase money transfers, and lose spacecraft, among other problems. The Gartner Group says the government will need to spend $30 billion, and 30 percent of its systems still won't be ready by January 1, 2000.

The Social Security Administration (SSA) is one agency that will be ready. It started making program changes in 1989 and will have completed them by December 31, 1998, leaving a full year to check out the code. Dean Mesterharm, deputy commissioner for systems, says the SSA will spend about $30 million on the changes.[22]

Telecommunications companies aren't faring much better. AT&T, which has five hundred million lines of code, began fixing programs in December 1996. It expects to be at that job for two years. Sprint is hiring an outside source to help with its one hundred million lines of code. It has already assigned six full-time and twenty part-time employees to do the work.[23]

A few phone calls to software vendors reveal that most of them are at least thinking about the year 2000 problem. Low-end accounting package vendor Peachtree says its DOS accounting systems are compliant, but its Windows accounting systems are not. High-end accounting system PeopleSoft Financials is year-2000-compliant.

■ ■ ■

Opportunities for CPAs

CPAs working in public practice as business consultants who advise clients on general operational issues should definitely include the year 2000 in their list. Some CPAs provide complete consulting services for companies wishing to outsource their year 2000 projects; others can advise companies just wishing to get a little project management guidance. The consulting arm of Gaines, Metzler, Kriner, and Company, LLP, GEMKO Information Group, Inc., provides a three-step approach to year 2000 projects:

1. Phase I: Assessment or Impact Analysis
2. Phase II: Strategy and Planning Phase
3. Phase III: Quality Assurance, Implementation, and Compliance Phase

According to a spokesperson, GEMKO positions year 2000 projects as opportunities for its customers to "renovate" their systems and achieve "long-term systems stability".

Coopers and Lybrand, LLP offers an information technology consulting program called Transition2000. Its Web site notes that it has completed projects for a major insurance company and a large financial services company.[24]

Information systems auditors can offer assurance services for existing systems' year 2000 status. CPAs can provide a number of consulting roles, including effectively running interference between a company and its

FIGURE 6.5: TIME IS TICKING TOWARD JANUARY 1, 2000

suppliers for interface compliance. They can also help to convince management of the magnitude of the problem if internal information systems staff has been unable to make progress on the issue.

"Audit teams get to walk into the boardroom," says Bill Wachel, senior manager of The Greentree Group and chairman of the Dallas-Fort Worth Prep 2000 Users Group. He believes the accounting and finance functions are poised to play a key role in promoting awareness of the year 2000 problem within senior management.

■ ■ ■

The End

The countdown continues . . you have less than one thousand days to go until 1/1/00.

ELECTRONIC COMMERCE

technology 7

Once a month, I acquiesce to the menial task of paying my bills. Lazily, I click on a list of vendors I pay each month, change the dollar amounts if necessary, and hit the send button. I then download my bank transactions. My checking account practically reconciles itself. I'm done with a thankless task in a few minutes. Even if bill-paying will never be remotely fun for some people, online banking and online bill payment have made it fast and cheap. You don't need expensive printed checks, you don't even need stamps, and you can get free software and free services from some banks.

I need to buy a book. A search at http://www.amazon.com reveals that they have it for $10 less than Border's, which is a fifteen-minute drive away. In just a few minutes, I add the book to my virtual shopping basket. It's on my front porch two days later.

My book purchase is baby stuff compared to the business-to-business commerce that is occurring on the Web. Cisco, which sells expensive, complicated network hardware, did $75 million in online business in its first five months.[1] AMP Inc., a $5 billion manufacturer of electronic components, receives thirty-three thousand hits per day on its AMP Connect site, a Web-based product catalog.[2]

Even a few CPAs are cashing in. John Lacher, a CPA who provides technology consulting services and who has been featured in the *Journal of Accountancy,* receives 100 percent of his revenues online.[3] Ernst and Young's new online consulting service for small businesses, called Ernie, generated over $1 million in 1996 for the seven months it was available.[4]

In 1996, online shopping sprees were expected to reach $5.4 billion, with significant growth foreseen through the end of the decade.[5] Currently, business-to-business commerce represents a hefty 81.5 percent of all Web commerce, and is expected to grow to 95.6 percent in 2000.[6]

This chapter discusses trends and best practices in electronic commerce, and is broken into the following sections:

1. Online banking
2. Consumer online commerce
3. Electronic payment options
4. Business online commerce
5. Web advertising
6. CPA online commerce
7. Issues and trends in electronic commerce

FIGURE 7.1: PROJECTED SALES ON THE WEB

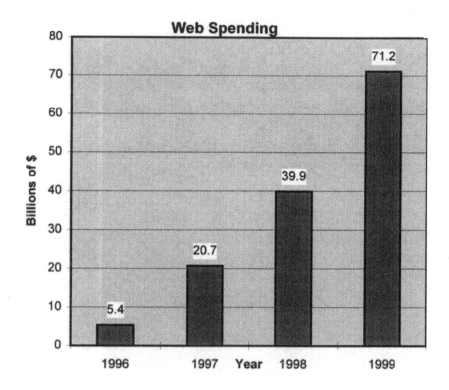

FIGURE 7.2: EXPECTED GROWTH IN BUSINESS-TO-BUSINESS WEB COMMERCE

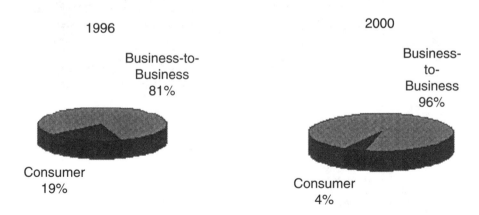

Before we go too far, let's define electronic commerce. Electronic commerce is business conducted between businesses or between businesses and individuals using a public network, such as the Internet, or a private network. It includes electronic shopping, online transactions, and electronic data interchange (EDI).[7] We'll defer our comments about EDI to Technology 10 and proceed with a discussion of our first topic, online banking.

ONLINE BANKING

Dozens of institutions are offering online banking, and some of them are offering it free of charge. Online banking consists of two primary components: online banking and online bill payment. Online banking refers to the ability to see account balances and to download transactions from the bank's computer to the consumer's computer. Online bill payment allows a consumer or business to pay bills electronically.

Online Banking

Exact details vary with each bank, but here are the general steps involved in online banking.

FIGURE 7.3: SEVERAL BANKS OFFER ONLINE BANKING FROM INTUIT'S QUICKEN ONLINE PAGE

1. You'll sign up with a bank that offers online banking. Depending on the bank, you'll receive a card (like an ATM card), personal identification number (PIN), and possibly a password. If you don't already have an account at this bank, you'll set it up at this time.

2. Different banks offer different access methods. Wells Fargo offers four choices for online banking: Intuit's Quicken, Microsoft's Money, Prodigy services, or its Internet site. Citibank has its own proprietary software called Direct Access, but you can also use Quicken. If you don't already have the software for the method you choose, you'll install it at this time.

3. When you're ready to bank, you'll dial in to the bank from your PC. You can see checking, savings, or credit card accounts. To receive a list of transactions that have cleared your account, you'll click on the download function and the transactions will be copied into your PC. Most banks will still send your monthly statement in the mail.

Online Bill Payment

An optional feature of online banking that also happens to be its most time-saving feature is online bill payment. After you have entered bills to be paid, you can "send" them to the bank. When the bank receives the bills, it pays them for you. You can pay anyone this way, from American Express to your local plumber. All you have to do is give the bank the person's name and address. The bank is responsible for tracking the person down and sending them your payment.

Behind this online bill payment service is a complicated network of agreements between thousands of players in the online community. When you pay your American Express bill from a Wells Fargo Bank, the payment is easily transferred from your account to American Express, which has an agreement with Wells Fargo. When you pay your plumber from your Citibank account, chances are Citibank does not yet have an agreement with your plumber. Citibank actually mails a cashier's check to your plumber and any others with whom it does not yet have an agreement. But the consumer is not inconvenienced. Citibank and other banks are aggressively signing up businesses for this network so that more and more businesses can easily receive online payments.

FIGURE 7.4: ONLINE BANKING WITH NATIONS BANK

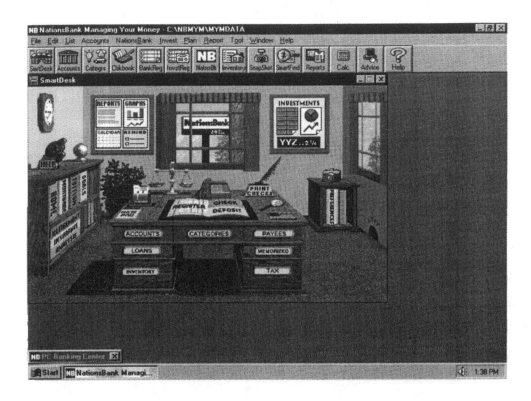

Benefits

Consumers and businesses that already have a PC and already keep track of their finances in Intuit's Quicken or Microsoft's Money are poised to gain from online banking. It takes about half the usual time to pay the bill online because there is nothing to print out, handle, stamp, and take to the mail room. The cost of office supplies, such as check forms and stamps, is eliminated. Businesses are more likely to receive their payments on time when a consumer can control which day the payment is to be processed.

Risks?

Are consumers and businesses worried about online security? Most people are. To do business on the Web, security precautions are imperative. Although the security for each Web site differs, most sites have installed the Secure Sockets Layer (SSL) encryption technology described in Technology 1. As the Secure Electronic Transaction (SET) standards are completed, companies will migrate to SET technology, which is more secure than SSL. A customer wishing to do business on the Web must use a secure browser, such as Microsoft Internet Explorer or Netscape Navigator, and the Web site must use a secure server. A consumer should never type a credit card number in an unsecured screen on the Web, such as an email or a form that is not on a secure server. (See Technology 1 for more information about security.)

Any online break-in is protected by the same laws as a paper forgery. The consumer is responsible only for notifying the bank as soon as he or she discovers any strange activity in his or her account. To address consumers' concerns about security, Wells Fargo devotes a portion of its Web site to explaining the technology features that provide security for its customers. At Citibank, a new-accounts representative has advised me that if you take normal precautions, online banking is at least as safe as or more safe than an ATM transaction. At least you have less chance of a stranger walking

FIGURE 7.5: WELLS FARGO EDUCATES CONSUMERS ABOUT WEB SECURITY

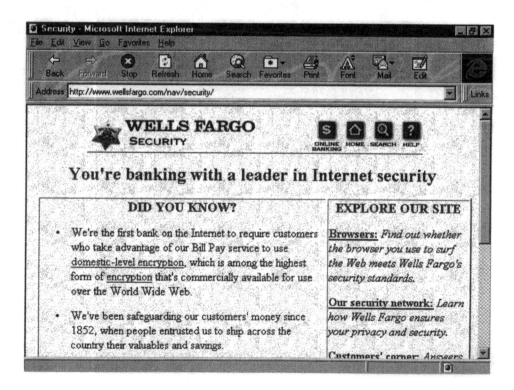

into the bedroom where your PC is and saying, "Give me all of your online cash!"

Many individuals are looking for a little assistance in getting their finances online. CPAs are ideally suited to offering the consulting services individuals are looking for. Offering services in online banking is a natural extension of tax preparation and personal financial planning services.

WHERE TO START ONLINE BANKING

A list of some of the banks that offer online banking appears below. If your bank does not appear in the list, check with its customer service department in case it has recently added the service.

American Express	1-800-AXP-7500
Bank of Boston	1-800-476-6262
Centura Bank	1-800-721-0501
Chase Manhattan Bank	1-800-CHASE24
Chemical Bank	1-800-CHEMBANK
Citibank	1-800-446-5331
Compass Bank	1-800-COMPASS
CoreStates Bank	1-800-562-6382
Crestar Bank	1-800-CRESTAR
First Chicago	1-800-800-8435
First Interstate Bank	1-800-YOU AND I
Home/Savings of America	1-800-310-4932
M&T Bank	1-800-790-9130
Marquette Banks/E Direct	1-800-708-8768
Michigan National Bank	1-800-CALL-MNB
Sanwa Bank California	1-800-23SANWA
Smith Barney	1-800-221-3636
SunTrust Bank	1-800-382-3232
Texas Commerce Bank	1-800-235-8522
Union Bank	1-800-796-5656
U.S. Bank	1-800-422-8762
Wells Fargo	1-800-423-3362 ext. Q

SOURCE: *Quicken Journal,* an insert in the Intuit *Quicken* software package.

■ ■ ■

Consumer Online Commerce

The topic of consumer electronic commerce is one that the press and writers like to criticize. Most consumers certainly have not caught on to the benefits of electronic purchasing. Roadblocks abound, including challenges in technology, consumer fears about security and privacy, and the good old human-being habit of resistance to change. Nevertheless, some companies are quietly making Web-prints into retail electronic commerce.

What Can You Buy on the Internet?

One site, touted by many consultants as the model for all online commerce, is a virtual bookstore. Self-described as "Earth's Biggest Bookstore," http://www.amazon.com allows its customers to order from its virtual inventory of one million titles. Most of the company's inventory resides in suppliers' warehouses, keeping its carrying costs very low. When I type "Walter Cronkite" into the site's search engine, a list of matches is

Figure 7.6: Buy a Book at Amazon.com

displayed, including Walter Cronkite's recent bestseller. I click on the title and see a picture of the cover, a description of the book, and the price. Anyone who has already read the book can enter a "book review" for all to see. There is even a feature for Walter Cronkite himself to comment on his own book. I click to put the book in my virtual shopping basket.

To purchase the book, I enter a secure server in which I enter my name and address. If I am a regular customer, I can enter an ID and a password, and my address information will not have to be rekeyed. If I am afraid to enter my credit card online, I can enter the last four digits and then call an 800 number to complete the transaction. An email confirms my order and provides shipping details.

The most significant feature of this site is that it gives the consumer a choice about how to complete the order. If a consumer is frightened by press reports about credit card safety online, he or she might go all the way through the order until asked for a credit card number, then stop. At Amazon, there is no pressure to put in the credit card number. So Amazon never loses a sale for this reason. If your firm plans to offer products and services over the Internet, consider giving customers an option to call and complete the sale the old-fashioned way. Until the mainstream accepts the Internet as a safe way to purchase items, giving consumers a choice will be the best option for ensuring maximum online sales for your firm.

The most popular online purchases include travel-related services and computer products. At http://www.dell.com, you can design your own PC and order it online. Dell saves labor when the consumer can tweak the configuration online rather than tie up a customer service representative's time figuring prices. The consumer saves time otherwise spent holding on a phone line. The consumer can also endlessly experiment with different configurations without feeling guilty about changing his or her mind and consuming the time of a customer-service representative.

Large retailers do not wish to be left out of the online odyssey. Wal-Mart is adding two hundred products per week to its Wal-Mart Online site. Electronics sell best, says a Wal-Mart customer service agent. Each order is shipped by UPS Ground service. Like Amazon, Wal-Mart gives the consumer a choice about entering a credit card number online or completing the transaction over the telephone.

Figure 7.7: Configure a Computer at Dell's Web Site

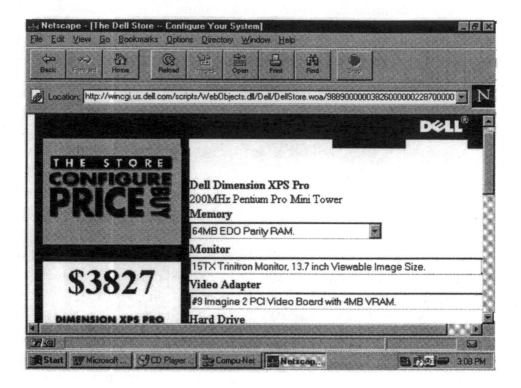

■■■
ELECTRONIC PAYMENT OPTIONS

Electronic Cash

A few businesses have ventured into using "electronic cash." To explain this concept, we'll use "ecash," one type of electronic cash created by a Netherlands company called DigiCash, that has offices in New York.[8] Please be aware that *ecash* is a registered trademark of the DigiCash company and not a generic name for electronic cash.

Ecash is stored on a person's computer disk, just as money is stored in a your pocket or purse. While surfing the Internet, you may want to spend cash at a particular site, for software or games, for example. You can pay for the software or games in ecash by transferring the ecash from your hard disk to the vendor's account.

Mark Twain Bank, in St. Louis, Missouri, is one of the few currently offering an ecash option. Both consumers and vendors can set up a special

FIGURE 7.8: ATTENTION WAL-MART SHOPPERS: THE ONLINE STORE IS
OPEN

type of bank account that will honor electronic cash disbursements and
collections.

A consumer who sets up an account with Mark Twain Bank can make
withdrawals from it to his or her PC. The ecash is stored on the PC's hard
disk in the form of electronic coins in many denominations. Just as a
person withdraws money from a checking account via an ATM
(automated teller machine), ecash can be withdrawn from an ecash account
and the ecash coins stored on the person's hard disk. As the coins are
needed in cyberspace, they can be transferred to friends or vendors or
redeposited into the bank. On the consumer's PC, software using graphics
includes commands to handle all of these types of transactions.

Vendors who accept ecash at their sites can store it on their computer or
deposit it directly into their ecash bank account. They may present a "bill"
or a request for payment to the consumer, which the consumer will
respond to using his or her ecash software. Vendors accepting ecash can
display a logo to alert consumers of this payment option.

Figure 7.9: Mark Twain Bank Offers Ecash

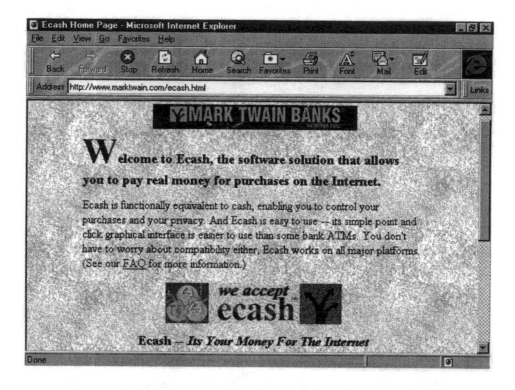

Figure 7.10: Web Sites That Offer Ecash

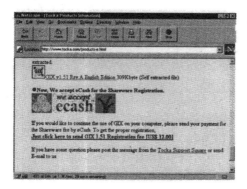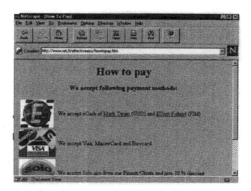

Standards have not yet been adopted for this type of technology, so other competing companies also offer various forms of electronic cash, namely CyberCash, which offers CyberCoins.

One word of warning to the CPA who decides to experiment with electronic payments: surfing the Internet with a hard disk full of electronic coins is like taking a walk on the mean streets of New Orleans with a wallet full of cash. You could get cyber-mugged by hackers who know how to acquire your coins. My advice: start with small change until you understand the nuances of the system.

Large issues loom over electronic cash, primarily because of the complexity of the technology involved in making this sort of system secure for all parties. Although it is worth experimenting with small denominations of electronic cash and even offering this payment alternative on a Web site, consumer acceptance of electronic cash will probably be slow and will not see any great gains in 1997.

Smart Cards

Another form of electronic commerce that is already widely accepted overseas is the smart card. The size of a credit card, a smart card has a chip that is recognized as cash by certain machines, such as pay telephones. Examples sold in Australia and Mexico are shown below.

PCs of the future will have smart-card readers built into their systems. This will enable many individuals to make online purchases with their smart cards. One of the companies pushing smart cards in this country is Mondex International, Inc., a joint venture of seven large companies, including AT&T, major banks, and credit card companies.

FIGURE 7.11: AUSTRALIA'S AND MEXICO'S PHONE CARDS: IT'S HARD TO PHONE HOME WITHOUT THEM

■ ■ ■

Business Online Commerce

Electronic commerce is hottest in the business-to-business sector. Quietly, and without the notice of the press, many businesses are setting up Web shops that cater to other businesses. Two leaders in this arena include Cisco and AMP.

Cisco Systems, Inc., a manufacturer of routers and switches for networks, introduced Cisco Connection Online in the summer of 1996. In its first five months, this site has registered eight thousand customers and produced $75 million in sales. Company officials hope to do 30 percent of Cisco's total sales, or $1.1 billion, via the site.[9]

Cisco's customers are attracted to the site because it helps them configure their networks and determine the components that they need to buy from Cisco. Cellular One, a Cisco customer, says it decided to increase its purchases from Cisco because of the pricing, order status information, and fast delivery that the Web site transaction offers.[10]

Not only does Cisco's site generate sales, it also reduces expenses. Selling, general, and administrative expenses are greatly reduced when customers can configure, order, and track their own purchases. By adding technical documentation to the site, Cisco estimates it has received thirty thousand fewer phone calls to its customer-support department. This translates into about $100 million in annual savings in customer support alone.[11]

AMP Connect is AMP Inc.'s Web catalog of products. AMP, a manufacturer of electronic components, sells over two hundred thousand products. About one-third of the products are available in the online catalog. Its catalog has been up since January 1996 and currently has thirty thousand registered users. One of the site's highlights is its search capabilities, which uses software provided by Saqqara Systems in Sunnyvale, California. The parametric search capability allows a user to find and compare products in the catalog. The success of the site has led AMP to launch a side business, AMP eMerce, which is a service that will help other Fortune 1000 manufacturers develop their Web sites.[12,13]

■ ■ ■

Web Advertising

One way to make money from your corporate Web site is to sell advertising space. You've probably seen advertising banners on search engines, online publications, entertainment sites, and software sites, where they are most common. Just as TV shows with the highest ratings get the best advertising, sites with the most traffic are raking in advertising revenues on the Internet.

Jupiter Communications, a market-research firm in New York, estimates that advertising revenue on the Internet will reach $5 billion by the year 2000. This will place Web ad revenues over radio ad revenues.[14]

CPA Online Commerce

A recent survey conducted by CCH, Inc. showed that there are many CPA firms with Web sites and many more planning to jump on in 1997:[15]

FIGURE 7.12: THE INFOSEEK WEB SITE IS A TOP EARNER IN WEB AD REVENUES

	On the Web (%)	Plan to Be on the Web in 1997 (%)
Big 6	100	100
Firms with more than ten employees	26	51
Firms with less than ten employees	3	13

Although the number of CPA firms actually engaged in electronic commerce is substantially less than these figures, some promising beginnings are apparent. A few sites offer online tax preparation. In a random search, I found one site that offered to answer tax questions for a flat fee per question.

Ernst & Young's Ernie, launched in 1996, offers online consulting services for small businesses. For a flat fee, Ernie subscribers can get answers to their questions from among twenty-one thousand Ernst & Young employees. Customers like it because they can present their what-if questions and do a little research before committing to a certain course of action. That course of action sometimes leads to more business for Ernst & Young, which is a nice side effect of the Ernie service.[16]

CPAs wishing to offer electronic commerce to their customers have a few choices including:

- They can build their own Web site. This will include constructing the forms needed for interaction with the customer and building the server infrastructure necessary to process the transactions securely.
- They can do business with one of the many enterprises that offer electronic storefronts. One example is IBM's World Avenue, where retailers can offer their goods online via a customized, interactive catalog in a secure environment.

Before a company decides to sell on the Web, it should consider the following:

1. Do not expect Web commerce to be a quick entry or a fast add-on to your business. The Web is a major marketing venue and businesses must strategize and plan how this line of business will integrate with their mainstream business.

2. Prepare a complete marketing plan, which includes such steps as identifying your market, your customers, and your competitors. The plan should answer questions such as—

    a. What type of customers will you attract on the Web, and how will they be different from your core customers?

    b. What is your competitive advantage?

3. Decide on the physical implementation and stick to a budget.

4. Integrate your Web site with your business systems. Connect the Web transactions and communications to your back office to maximize productivity and seamlessness. [17]

5. Think outside the box. At its finest, selling on the Web can provide new ways of doing business. Federal Express made headlines last year with its package-tracking sites. Its online mastery has opened up new revenue sources that were not even dreamed about earlier. Federal Express now sells logistics services, which include managing the ordering and delivery function for some businesses. Monorail, Inc., a PC distributor in Atlanta, relies on FedEx to take its customers' orders and handle the deliveries. Monorail bypasses expensive middlemen and keeps inventories low using the arrangement with FedEx. [18]

■ ■ ■

ISSUES AND TRENDS

Several roadblocks threaten to slow the growth of electronic commerce. Security is certainly utmost in everyone's mind and is fully discussed in Technology 1. Taxation is another issue that tends to confuse people easily. We'll explore it, and then we'll look at auditing issues and the new trend of offering personalized sites.

Taxability of Online Transactions

Twenty percent of finance executives do not know whether their company's Internet sales are taxable or not, according to a poll run by KPMG in 1996. Most companies are confused by existing tax laws and how they should be applied to online commerce. The poll also found that 90 percent of the companies want the government to clarify tax requirements. [19]

In December 1996 the White House did, in fact, describe its electronic policy in a twenty-three page report. Of taxation, it stated that existing tax concepts and principles should be followed, and taxation, in general, should be kept simple.[20] The complete document can be found at http://www.iitf.nist.gov/electronic_commerce.htm.

In February 1997 Senator Ron Wyden (D-Oregon) and Representative Chris Cox (R-California) were expected to introduce legislation that would stop states from levying taxes on Internet commerce.[21]

Audit Issues

The primary issues when auditing a company that engages in electronic commerce over the Internet are its lack of paper documentation and its unique source of orders. An auditor who is trained to perform audits in an EDP environment will be more comfortable dealing with this environment than an auditor who is not trained in performing computer-based audits. Two of the special considerations for electronic commerce are—

FIGURE 7.13: THE WHITE HOUSE'S ELECTRONIC COMMERCE POLICY

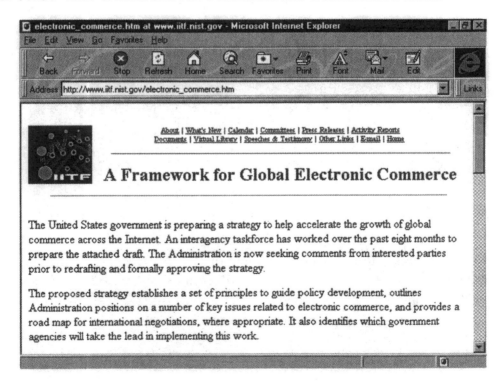

1. Identifying all entry points for transaction initiation to assess the scope of the system, the electronic audit trail, and the system's controls.

2. Paying special attention to automated control and security features that bridge the Internet and the corporate systems.

Personalized Sites

Just about all of the Web sites that were online as of the end of 1996 offered the same pages for everyone. You would see the same pages that I would see when visiting any particular site. But a very small movement, called personalized sites, is afoot. It may significantly enhance our Web experience. [22]

Some of this is already happening. Any site with a search engine quickly allows us to find what we are looking for. Any online bank will present customized, personal bank account balances and transaction information. Any site with an agent will present you with personal information it has learned about you from information that you have previously submitted. (For example, Firefly, described in Technology 4, lists movies it thinks I might enjoy.)

But think about it one step further. What if a site showed you the items it thought you were most likely to buy? Fingerhut Corporation, a catalog retailer, has designed such a site, which is scheduled to premier the first quarter of 1997. The Illinois Chamber of Commerce is planning a recruitment and job-search site that will be customizable. Virgin Net, a British conglomerate, is promising to get into the act as well. [23]

Will CPAs get into the act of customized sites? We'll be watching for it, online.

WORKFLOW TECHNOLOGY

technology 8

"Wow, I'm pretty impressed with our new bank. I called them this morning about a small loan, and by noon the money was in our checking account."

"When my car got damaged by hail, I was worried about the hassle. But I drove to the insurance company's claims center, and thirty minutes later I had a check for $3,200 in my hand."

"I hate getting my taxes done because last year my CPA kept my records for five months. But this year, when I went to a new firm, they scanned in my records, and I got to take my originals home with me. And they finished my return in a week."

These companies have a competitive edge. They can deliver their services faster than their competition. What is the secret? The work horses behind the scenes in these companies are workflow systems.

Workflow technology is software that enables information to be moved and processed among individuals in a group. It can be done with any number of technologies, so implementing workflow systems can encompass a lot of the other technologies discussed in this book. For example, workflow systems are often integrated with image processing systems. Image processing technologies were discussed in Technology 2.

Because the definition of work flow is so broad, technologies such as email qualify as primitive types of workflow systems. Although this chapter discusses the breadth of workflow systems, it focuses on traditional workflow systems, which are business process workflow systems. The chapter is organized into the following sections:

1. The business case for workflow.
2. Types of workflow systems.
3. Trends in workflow systems.

■ ■ ■
THE BUSINESS CASE FOR WORK FLOW

It used to take three weeks to assemble a one hundred-twenty-thousand-page federal drug-approval application at Solvay Human Health, a drug manufacturer. With a new workflow system, it now takes two hours. The systems runs on two Hewlett-Packard servers on a TCP/IP (Transmission Control Protocol/Internet Protocol)-based LAN (local area network) running Windows-based clients. The workflow software was custom-built on top of Documentum Inc.'s Enterprise Document Management System.[1]

Consolidated Edison has implemented a workflow system that identifies accounting and billing exceptions. The system is LAN-based and accepts scanned documents and faxes as well as mainframe-based exception reports. Although the system cost $1 million to develop, it eliminated the clerical labor of report distribution and review, and will generate a return in its first year.[2]

It used to take two working days to record, abstract, and index the paperwork that accompanies the sale of a property in Essex County, Massachusetts. Because a client/server-based workflow system was installed, the process now takes five minutes. The work force was reduced by 25 percent, and the smaller staff handles three times as many documents. Bookbinding costs of $90,000 per year were saved, too. The agency runs Unisys' InfoImage document-management system on a Unisys server. An Oracle relational database, an imaging system from Sigma Imaging Systems, and a FileNet jukebox constitute the system. Employees access the system via DOS and Windows PCs on a Novell NetWare LAN.[3]

USAir has a paperwork challenge relating to 1.7 million pages of airplane maintenance manuals, training documents, and engineering orders. USAir sends updates to a technical publishing group that customizes the documents to the airline's standards. The customized documents are sent out to the field for comments. All of the changes must be coordinated, reviewed, and approved. If a document misses a routing, a flight could be canceled because of a repair snafu. The $9 million workflow system USAir has adopted will cut the review process from three months to less than two weeks and save the company $10.5 million annually. The system will run on Unix machines.[4]

You can see how diverse workflow technology is. It solves a multitude of problems for a variety of entities. The benefits of workflow technologies are as follows:

- *Savings in labor and productivity.* Some companies experience a *tremendous* savings in labor and productivity.
- *Competitive advantage.* Customer service improves when questions are answered faster or service calls are streamlined. Products can reach market sooner.
- *Enforcement of business rules.* The workflow system sees to it that procedures are followed, reducing costly errors.

■ *Processes are reengineered and streamlined.* Companies that model and re-engineer their processes before implementing workflow systems are more successful with workflow technologies than companies that do not perform these steps. Business processes that were performed previously that do not add value to a process can be eliminated.

■ *Effective utilization of resources.* A good workflow system can move work among desks, even if the desks are in different cities. A paper-based system is inflexible if there is a workload imbalance at offices located in two different cities.

The costs of workflow systems are difficult to quantify because the solutions are so diverse. Often, the costs run into the millions of dollars. Generally, the costs will include—

■ *Incremental hardware.* To implement a workflow system, you must have a network. (Technology 9 discusses networks.) You will most likely need an imaging system as well. (Technology 2 discusses imaging system.) The exact hardware required for workflow implementation will vary by project. Some examples are listed below for consideration.
   — Additional workstations or additional servers may be required.
   — The cost of increased bandwidth across a network must be included in a workflow budget, as the flow of documents and work will generate more traffic on the network.
   — The cost of increased storage required by the workflow documents should be factored into the workflow budget.

■ *Software.* Software costs include the cost of a package, the cost to customize it, and the cost to implement it. The cost to customize the workflow system can be ongoing. As businesses continually change their processes, the workflow system must adapt. Software maintenance agreements and the legal costs of executing a contract should be included as well.

■ *Training and user support.* The users of the system must be trained to use the new package. Generally, a workflow system causes a major change in how workers perform their jobs. The task of training cannot be overlooked. A help desk facility is useful for questions that occur after the initial phase.

■ *Technical support and maintenance.* Like any other software system, the workflow system must be managed by systems professionals.

Some companies stay away from workflow installations because the systems are difficult to develop and manage.[5] Workflow is not for the faint of heart. A workflow system that encompasses the entire corporation can take nine to fifteen months to implement, on average.[6] The types of companies that could experience a high payback from workflow systems tend to be companies with one or more of the following characteristics:

1. *Paper-intensive processes.* This includes many service-based businesses. Banks (loan applications), insurance companies (claims processing), and CPA firms (tax returns) are examples of firms that can streamline and speed their paper flows with workflow systems.

2. *Collaborative processes.* This includes companies working on long, complicated documents that involve many approval steps. Lawyers working on cases with multiple documents such as depositions, evidence exhibits, and other court documents can use a workflow system to gather comments from all the parties involved. By using a workflow system, CPAs working on consulting projects can collaborate with team members on project documents.

3. *Tight or competitive deadlines.* Workflow systems speed processing of paperwork for companies with deadlines for bids, product development, or project delivery.

Companies that are new to workflow software should consider implementing workflow in small pilot projects. The pilot projects can work out the "bugs" more efficiently in a small group before the workflow system is rolled out to the entire organization.

■ ■ ■
Types of Workflow Systems

Because of workflow's broad definition, there are a number of software systems that are considered to be workflow systems. They range from the simple to the complex, and it is useful to categorize them into three major groups.

1. Low-end workflow systems

2. Groupware systems

3. Business process workflow systems

The first two categories of workflow systems are also referred to as *workgroup* systems.

Low-End Workflow Systems

Two primary groups of software are considered in this category of simple workflow software: email and forms management software. Some analysts say that these software packages should not be considered workflow systems, but they are included here to give you the broadest possible picture of workflow technologies.

Many CPAs are already benefiting from the powerful productivity offered by email. Via email messages, employees receive directions from bosses, reports from subordinates, and broadcast messages about company activities. The workflow activities in an email system are limited to routing messages and work. Email systems are more fully discussed in Technologies 4 and 9.

Forms management software is another type of very simple workflow software. This software enables the user to construct, customize, and use a lot of different types of forms. Packages like Delrina's FormFlow and Jetform are in this category.[7]

Groupware

Groupware provides electronic collaboration tools that enable groups of people to complete projects faster. Groupware systems provide messaging and project document management. Documents about a project can be stored, viewed, edited, and approved by individuals in the project group. Individuals can create, route, and reply to messages within a project or within an enterprise, depending on the groupware product.

Lotus Notes is the quintessential groupware product. There's still not really anything quite like Notes on the market. The two packages that come close are Microsoft Exchange and Novell GroupWise. Both of these products are messaging-based, whereas Notes is designed around a database structure.

Lotus Notes

Companies using Notes must build custom applications for each project. The applications are built around a project database, which holds documents about the project. The project team members can create, route, edit, annotate, and approve the project documents. Users can send messages about the project. Remote and Internet access are also available in Notes.

Lotus Notes is widely used. Two examples follow:

1. A Seattle insurance company saves labor and office expense from a Lotus Notes application that allows a major customer to view claims online.[8]

2. A Washington legal firm uses Lotus Notes for collaboration among lawyers and clients on contract work. The lawyers were sheepish at first about posting their work-in-progress, but the system caught on when the firm saved significantly on clerical support, office expense, floor space, and filing cabinets.[9]

Microsoft Exchange and Novell GroupWise

Exchange and GroupWise focus on message creation and support document routing. Documents can be created, routed, edited, and annotated by team members.[10] To enforce workflow rules about document processing and document flow, custom software must be programmed or third-party software packages that run on top of Exchange or Groupwise purchased.

Exchange is good at messaging and routing. Its use of folders and similar look to Windows Explorer make managing an individual's in-box easy. Third-party software has been developed to strengthen Exchange's workflow and collaborative functions. Some companies that have developed workflow products that run on top of Exchange include Keyfile Corporation, Reach Software, Inc., FileNet Corporation (Ensemble product), and Ultimus. Microsoft's Outlook (in Microsoft Office '97) client provides collaborative features for Exchange. Some information systems managers agree that using one of these products is better than designing custom applications in Visual Basic (programming language) to support forms and document workflow in Exchange.[11]

FIGURE 8.1: WEB PAGE FOR LOTUS NOTES

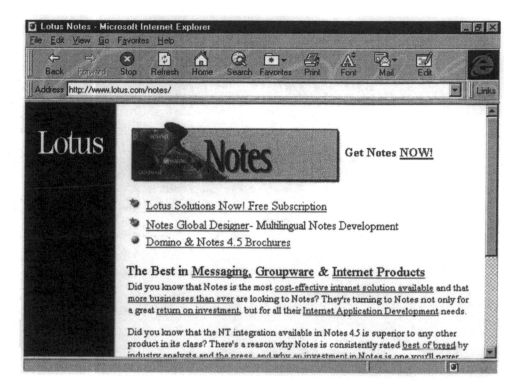

GroupWise borrows from NetWare's directory services to provide a global and personal address book. Although messaging-based, it includes a document-management system. The calendaring and scheduling features are quite rich. Email and telephone messages can be integrated, and an NLM (NetWare Loadable Module) called Web Access allows a user to listen to his or her voice messages (which have been turned into **.wav** files) from a Web browser. A workflow add-on helps to automate the routing of documents.[12]

Business Process Workflow Systems

A business process workflow system automates a set of business processes in a structured, rules-oriented format. Some of the business processes that can be automated include expense report processing, loan application processing, and capital appropriation request processing.

Workflow systems are designed around a set of business activities. A business activity is a step in a business process, such as "check bank references on loan application" or "send completed loan application to

FIGURE 8.2: MICROSOFT EXCHANGE'S MAIN SCREEN

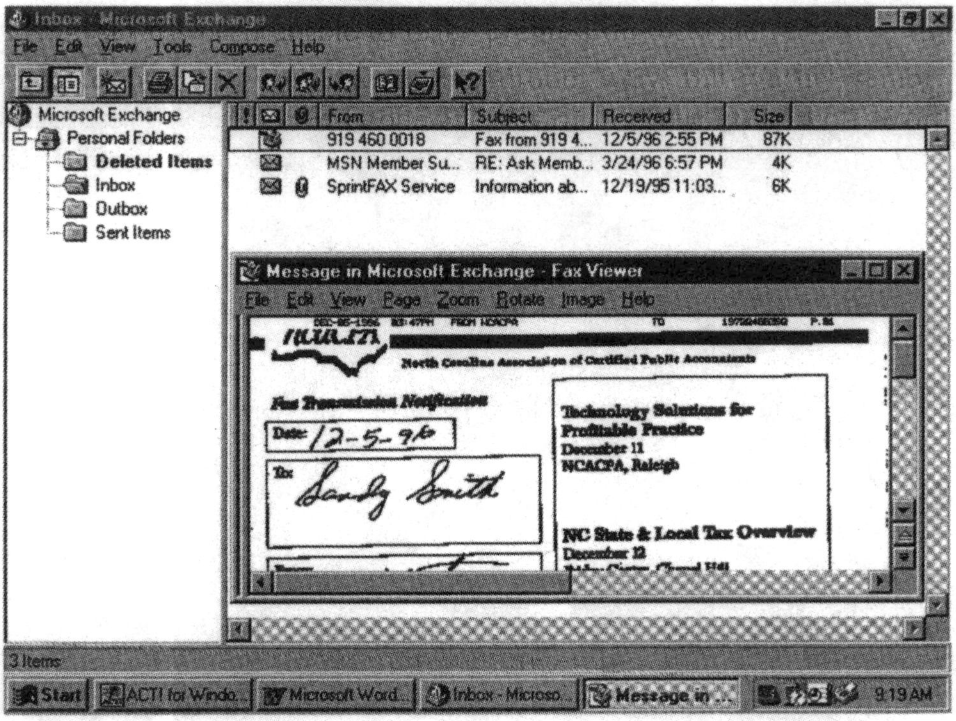

loan officer". A workflow system designer will determine the order of each activity, what information is required at each activity, and how exceptions will be handled at each activity. This information constitutes a business process that is then automated using the workflow tools.

Routing

Routing the documents is a major function of a workflow system. Any document that must be routed for comments or approval is an excellent application for workflow. A document or set of documents will be "placed in" an electronic envelope that is routed by a workflow system. Workflow systems vary as to what types of documents they can handle, but the most flexible systems handle a variety of types, including word processing text, multimedia graphics, sound clips, and even video clips.

The electronic envelope of documents is routed from workstation to workstation according to a set of predefined rules. For example, if an expense report is ready for manager approval, the envelope containing the expense report and supporting documents can be routed to the manager for approval.

Workflow systems can also handle exceptions when they come up. If a document needs to be routed to a specialist, the workflow software can find the specialist and route the document accordingly. If a workstation in Denver is overloaded with documents waiting to be processed and a workstation in Seattle is idle, the workflow system can reroute the Denver load to the Seattle desk.

Rules

As the document passes each station or step, the workflow system checks to see if processing rules have been met. If all rules have been met, the document can go on to the next station. If the rules have not been met, the system will flag the exceptions and notify the worker. For example, before the expense report can be sent to a manager for approval, it should contain supporting documents, be signed by the originator, and include account codes.

A large part of the installation of a workflow system is getting the rules set up in the system. Each participant of the system must be interviewed to determine what the rules will be for a particular process being automated. Then the rules must be input into the system. The users of the new system must be trained in the rules of the process and in the workflow system itself.

Regarding the setup of the rules in a medium-sized CPA firm that automated its tax process, Eric McMillen, systems consultant at Boomer Consulting, Inc., says, "The biggest challenge was not the hardware or software setup, it was the design and implementation of the workflow. The workflow problems stemmed from the fact that no two partners had the same system for the handling of files and workpapers."

Business processes in most companies are very fluid. The most usable workflow systems make it easy to change business process rules and employee roles. Modifying workflow rules is an ongoing part of workflow systems. As companies learn more about the processes that are being performed through the workflow systems, they'll change the rules to improve the processes.

Applications Systems Integration

Once that expense report is completed and approved by all necessary parties, wouldn't it be nice if one more button could be pushed to send it to accounts payable? Many workflow systems include the capability of being integrated with a company's application systems. Most often, the interface must be custom-programmed. The seamlessness provided with such capabilities adds significant productivity to the business process being automated.

As workflow software matures, we will see more integration among business systems. The workflow system will carry the work to a certain point in a process, then it will call in an applications system to perform a task, after which the workflow system may take the work further down the line and pass it to another application system. The work gets done in a streamlined, fully automated environment. The system that's best for the task at hand gets called in to do its part in the work process.

Document Tracking

Workflow systems can track the status or whereabouts of a set of documents. The systems can answer questions such as—

- "Where is Jane's expense report?"
- "What approvals are we waiting for on the Smith project?"
- "How many days does it take us to service a customer?"
- "On average, how long does a customer have to wait before we answer the call?"

The tracking feature of a workflow system can lead to increased customer service and a competitive edge for businesses.

Business Process Reengineering

Companies that implement workflow applications find that business process reengineering is a natural step to take before a workflow system is implemented. Business process reengineering forces a company to "clean up" its processes before automating them. A company saves big in two ways:

1. It cuts out unnecessary redundant processes.
2. It automates the remaining, necessary processes.

Businesses that reengineer their processes before implementing a workflow system tend to gain more in productivity than businesses that do not reengineer.

Vendors and Products

A few workflow companies and their products include—[13]

- IBM—FlowMark.
- InConcert—InConcert.
- FileNet—Visual WorkFlo.
- Wang—OPEN/workflow.
- Cincom—TOTAL FrameWork.
- Action Technologies, Inc.—Metro.
- Staffware—Staffware.
- Logical Software Solutions—FlowMan.

FIGURE 8.3: WEB PAGE FOR WANG OPEN/WORKFLOW PRODUCT

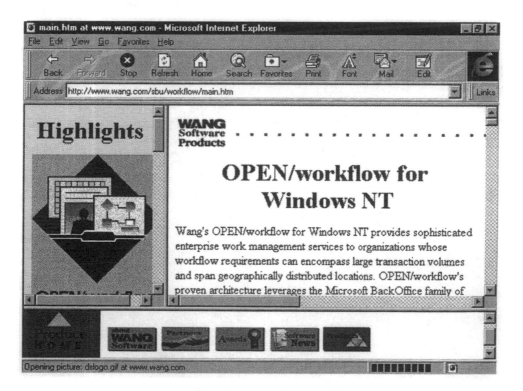

These products provide graphic design tools, screen builders, rules scripting, and distributed-enterprise capabilities.

■ ■ ■
Trends in Workflow Systems

A recent *Computerworld* article about workflow listed ten trends that are affecting the market for workflow products:[14]

1. Business process reengineering (already briefly discussed in this chapter)

2. A move to standards-based software (discussed next in this section)

3. Integration of imaging capabilities with applications (discussed in Technology 2)

4. Ubiquitous computers

5. A desire for a paperless office

6. Migration to a client/server environment

7. The growing popularity of optical character recognition (discussed in Technology 2)

8. Low software prices

9. Vendor consolidation

10. Improved connectivity among workflow systems

In addition to the issue of standards, three other topics will be presented in this section:

1. Off-the-shelf workflow software

2. Workflow systems outside of imaging

3. Workflow and intranets

A Need for Standards

The lack of common terminology among workflow vendors is confusing to workflow customers. The lack of interoperability among interfacing systems, such as document-management, imaging, database, and email systems, is a challenge, to say the least. The Workflow Management Coalition was formed to develop standards for the workflow industry as well as a common glossary of workflow terms.

Off-the-Shelf Workflow Software

One of the disadvantages of implementing workflow systems is the high amount of customization required to develop them. Vendors that can provide drag-and-drop workflow design will solve this problem.

PaperClip Software Inc. adds to its DMS (document-management system) product by offering PaperClip Workflow. This product implements rules-based processing in a graphic interface. The product is a very low-end workflow system, but it's a start in the direction of easier customization.[15]

Workflow Systems Outside of Imaging

You can design a workflow system without using workflow software at all. The Readers' Digest Association did. In a system that handles printing bids from design to purchasing to accounts payable, the company used email, an SQL (Structured Query Language) database, and spreadsheets.[16]

A workflow system does not have to be tied to a document-management system. The concept of workflow can be widely applied to any paperwork

FIGURE 8.4: WEB PAGE FOR PAPERCLIP WORKFLOW PRODUCT

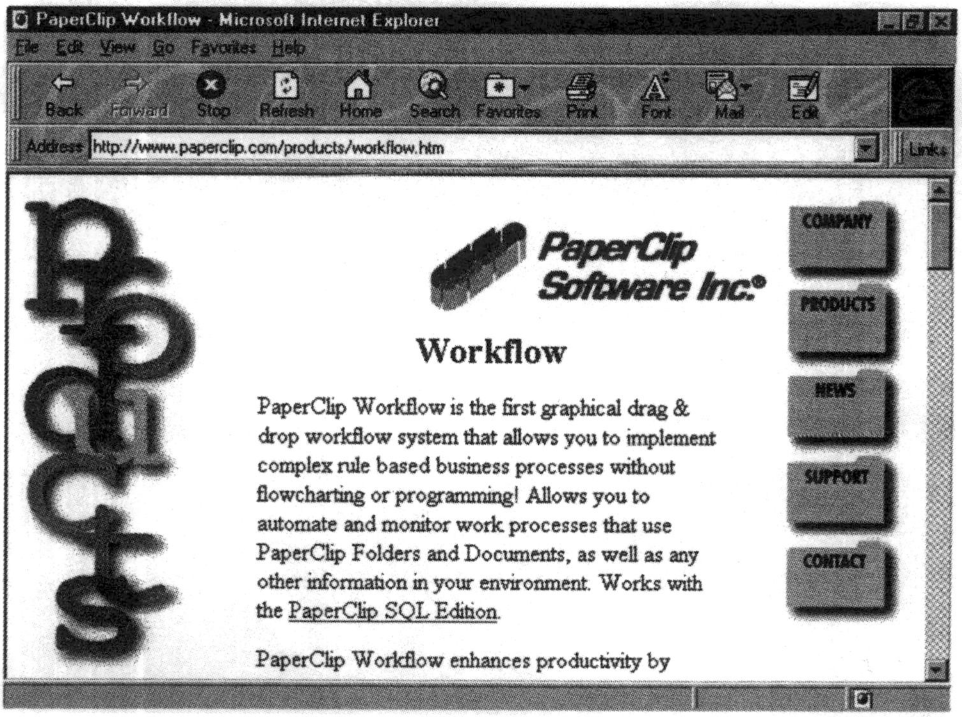

process in the company. The most effective applications will be those that use both information and individuals most effectively.

Workflow and Intranets

Intranets, which are companies' internal networks that use Web technologies, are great tools for document distribution. So it's only natural that workflow enters the intranet picture as well. Eli Lilly uses Netscape's Navigator, a browser, to view documents stored in its document-management system. By clicking on a hypertext link, drug researchers can answer Food and Drug Administration questions online instead of paging through thick paper manuals. The system helps Eli Lilly make decisions faster, which gets products to market faster.[17]

Although Eli Lilly custom-developed its own code for the link between Microsoft Word documents and the intranet, there are products available to take advantage of Internet technologies. Documentum produces Accelera, its Internet interface. Novasoft offers NovaWeb, its Web server.[18] Action Technologies offers Internet integration through its Metro line of products.[19]

Intranets are covered more fully in Technology 9.

PRIVATE NETWORKS

technology 9

If you've been using computers for at least a decade, you'll likely remember VisiCalc. When this popular spreadsheet package first appeared nearly twenty years ago, it was the greatest thing since sliced bread. Accountants quickly got rid of those oversized, stodgy ledger sheets and let the computer foot and balance numbers.

Pretty soon, everyone in the office was using a computer. PCs and Macs proliferated quickly because of packages just like VisiCalc. But that presented a new problem: now VisiCalc files needed to be shared. So SneakerNet was invented: put the file on a floppy diskette, walk the floppy over to the co-worker who needed to see the VisiCalc file, and let the co-worker view or copy the file. SneakerNet wasn't very productive, but it was the best available at the time. In fact, SneakerNet is still a mission-critical application in some CPA firms.

Others have moved up from SneakerNet and connected their PCs via a network. A network can consist of as few as two PCs or as many as thousands. Users of PCs on a network can communicate with each other when the PCs are connected. They can even share each other's VisiCalc files, if there are any old ones that still exist.

The mother of all networks is the Internet, which is a public network. Access to public networks is open to anyone willing to pay the access fee. We discussed the Internet and public networks in Technology 4.

Private networks, our number 9 technology and the topic of this chapter, are nonpublic networks that are used by employees and maybe select customers. Access to private networks is restricted to authorized users only. (A special type of private network, the intranet, is the hottest thing around these days. Intranets are discussed in the last part of the chapter.)

FIGURE 9.1: THE HORSEPOWER BEHIND SNEAKERNET

This chapter presents

1. The business case for networking.
2. Some networking concepts and terminology.
3. Management and administrative issues of networking.
4. Trends in network operating systems.
5. Intranets.

One point of clarification: we'll probably use the term "networked computers." That term does not mean the same thing as the term "network computers." Network computers, or NCs, are hardware devices that are less expensive than PCs and limited in their functionality. This chapter reserves its discussion of clients to PCs and other desktop systems like Apple MacIntosh; NCs will not be discussed.

■ ■ ■
THE BUSINESS CASE FOR NETWORKING

Companies can significantly benefit from networking their PCs. Most large companies have complicated network configurations. Even small companies with just two or three computers can profit from networking their PCs.

Mom Always Said to Share

First, networks allow resources to be shared. Resources, such as hardware, software, and files, can be used by any of the people on the network. A company with five employees and five computers might have to buy five printers if the PCs are not networked. If the PCs are networked, the company can buy one printer and install it on the network. All five employees can access the one printer from the network. The same thing applies to hard drives: a large network drive can hold files that are shared among employees. Other peripherals, such as scanners, can be hooked into a network and shared in the same way.

Software can be shared as well. A network license for a software package is almost always priced more economically than individual copies. Plus, some licenses allow you to buy for concurrent usage instead of total usage. When buying a concurrent license, the software may be available to ten people, but if only three are using it at any one time, you need to buy only three licenses. Additionally, a network can be a useful tool in distributing and updating software files.

Files that are stored on a network drive can also be shared among network users. This capability greatly increases the potential of collaboration among employees on the network.

Mom Always Said to Write

In addition to resource sharing, another great feature of networks is email. Employees can send messages to one another. The messages stay in a file on the server until the employee checks his or her electronic mail box. In the days I spent working for Fortune 100 companies, I found that using email instead of phone calls boosted my productivity significantly. I could fire off twenty email messages in the time it would have taken me to complete three phone calls.

A Foundation for Bigger Things

The network is just the beginning. It provides the technical foundation for many applications that improve the effectiveness of the organization's employees. Collaboration software like Lotus Notes must be run on a network. A report distribution system must be run on a network. Client/ server applications must be run on a network. Companies that have the foundation that networks provide will be able to run these additional applications.

Costs

The major costs of networks include—

- Hardware, including servers, network cards, and other components.
- Cabling.
- Software, including the network operating system and utilities.
- Installation labor for first-time installation, upgrades, and employee moves.
- Labor to administer and manage the network.
- Help desk support, if there is no separate end-user computing function.

For nearly ten years, Gartner Group has helped organizations track the cost of owning and managing a network. Their TCO (total cost of ownership) model shows that, assuming a three-year life for hardware, *each* networked

PC costs $13,200 per year. This figure includes hardware, software, support, administrative services, and end-user operations.[1]

The ongoing costs of managing and administering a network are a significant component of total network costs. A recent study by Business Research Group focuses on these costs alone. They asked 240 LAN (local area network) administrators to consider administration costs, task time, and ease of use. The results were tallied by type of operating system and are shown in Table 9.1.[2]

TABLE 9.1: COSTS OF NETWORK OWNERSHIP

	Sites With Less Than 100 Servers		Sites With More Than 100 Servers	
	Per Server	*Per Client*	*Per Server*	*Per Client*
Windows NT	$10,167	$1,017	$4,076	$123
NetWare	$11,729	$ 757	$4,839	$202
OS/2 Warp	$ 8,310	$ 782	$3,584	$ 53

Downtime

Remember the mainframe days? We used dumb terminals to get to our programs and data on the mainframe. We sometimes waited and waited for a response. Then the whole enchilada would go down, and we would see how close to lunchtime it was.

An engineer friend remarked to me lately how networks are getting just as bad. One of the goals of moving from mainframes to networks was the hope for more independence from the central machine. But when all your work is on the server, you're still dependent on that one central machine.

Successful businesses will recognize that this issue can easily be managed. Employees want to be given tools that will make them the most productive. A reliable network and a backup plan in case of unforeseen failure will ensure that your employees are not saying the same thing as my engineer friend (who, ironically, works for one of the largest makers of PCs).

■ ■ ■

SOME NETWORKING CONCEPTS AND TERMINOLOGY

LAN

LAN is the acronym for a local area network that connects a group of people in a small company or department. PCs connected to a LAN are geographically close together, generally in the same building or even on the same floor. A company can have many LANs. There can be an accounting LAN, a marketing LAN, and so forth.

Most LANs are organized in a client/server architecture. A client is a PC, and many clients will be connected to a LAN. A server is a machine that coordinates the network activity and runs software called a network operating system. Examples of network operating systems include Novell NetWare, Windows NT Server, OS/2 Warp Server, and Banyan Vines.

There are many types of servers, depending on what functions are performed via the network. Examples include file servers, print servers, database servers, application servers, remote access servers, and Internet servers. Any one LAN can have any number of servers doing their particular jobs on the network. It's common to name servers after a group of like items; one of my customers has named them after mountains: McKinley, Rainier, and Kilimanjaro.

WANs (Wide Area Networks) and MANs (Metropolitan Area Networks)

LANs and PCs can be connected to each other in a network called a wide area network (WAN). A WAN can connect the accounting department LAN on one floor with the marketing department LAN on another. Or a WAN can connect LANs and PCs across the state or country.

One more acronym you might see occasionally is MAN (metropolitan area network). A MAN will connect machines in one town or geographical area.

Components of a Network

Cable

The PCs that are connected in a network are physically connected by cable (except for wireless networks). There are four primary types of cable:

FIGURE 9.2: DRIVES AVAILABLE TO A PC CONNECTED TO A NETWORK

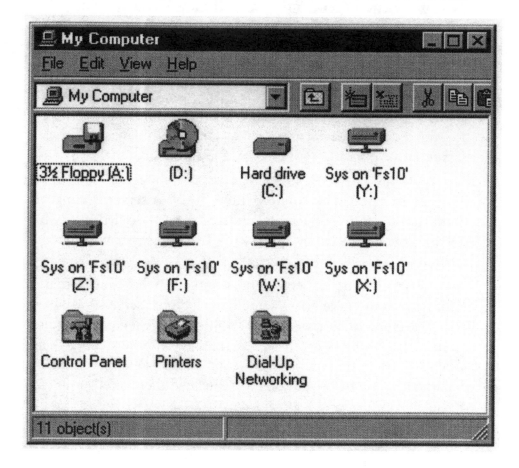

1. Unshielded twisted pair (UTP)
2. Shielded twisted pair (STP)
3. Coaxial cable (coax)
4. Fiber

The cable runs from the PC to the server through a connection point, such as a hub or a multi-station access unit (MAU).

Most companies will cable with UTP because of its low cost and flexibility. On the other end, fiber will be used by companies with extraordinary needs. DreamWorks, a Hollywood production company, has a fiber network, probably because of its need for multimedia communications. Coax and STP are rarely used for new installations.

FIGURE 9.3: A TYPICAL NETWORK

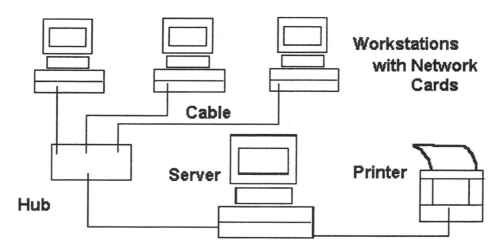

Physical Network Options

Each PC must be equipped with a network card (or, more properly, a network interface card, or NIC) that fits into an open slot in the computer. The network card provides the connection for the cable, which joins the PC to the network.

Ethernet is the most popular type of network card. Ethernet is available in speeds of 10Mbps (10BaseT) and 100Mbps (100BaseT). IBM Token Ring is another type of network card and is used primarily by companies that are heavily invested in IBM equipment. There was a time when Token Ring was considered the superior technology, while Ethernet was better for small networks and less expensive. Today Ethernet technology has overcome any theoretical advantages that Token Ring had and continues to be less expensive.

The difference between Ethernet and Token Ring is in how they handle traffic over the network. Ethernet is based on collision detection (CSMA/CD, or Carrier Sense Multiple Access/Collision Detection), whereas IBM Token Ring is based on collision avoidance (CSMA/CA, or Carrier Sense Multiple Access/Collision Avoidance). To illustrate the difference, let's take a group of people in a room. When two people try to talk at once, one person will stop, and the other person will begin talking. It's the same with traffic on an Ethernet network: colliding packets will yield to each other, and one will go ahead of the other. In contrast, traffic on a Token Ring network needs "permission" before it can go. In a meeting of people, this would be similar to having a meeting leader call on each person before the person could talk.

Protocols

Most CPAs will never need to know the intricacies of network protocols, but should nonetheless know the names as well as which networks support which protocols.

■ *IPX.* Internetwork Packet Exchange, or IPX, is NetWare's protocol that handles routing, addressing, and packets. Microsoft Windows NT also supports IPX.

■ *TCP/IP.* Transmission Control Protocol/Internet Protocol, or TCP/IP, is the Internet protocol. It is a standard that allows machines from multiple platforms to share and transfer data with each other. Microsoft Windows NT uses TCP/IP. Novell now offers TCP/IP also, through its IntranetWare product, which is included in the latest version of NetWare.

VLAN (Virtual LAN)

A VLAN, or virtual LAN, is a grouping of client machines within a LAN that have a common project or a reason to be grouped. The grouping is done through software instead of through hardware and cables. Companies with individuals who move from project to project are good candidates for using the VLAN configuration. Companies with individuals who are geographically dispersed but working on the same project are also good candidates for a VLAN because of the efficient way VLANs handle traffic within the group.

Networking the Networks With Bridges, Routers, and Gateways

A bridge is hardware that connects networks that use the same protocol. Bridges sort all the traffic on the network. A router is hardware that will be placed at the intersection of the LANs. Routers select the route for network traffic. A gateway is hardware that links networks with different protocols, such as a LAN and a mainframe.

These hardware components act as the traffic cops of a network, directing data traffic from one part of a network to another. You may also see the term *brouters,* which are hybrids between bridges and routers. If it sounds like bridges, routers, and gateways have overlapping features, you're right.

The features of bridges, routers, and gateways have become more difficult to distinguish as networks and their components have become more complex.

Good Things Come in Small Packets

Data travels over networks in packets. A word processing file, for example, is broken up into packets. Packets have a special layout that the network can recognize and direct to its correct destination. A packet looks like this:

FIGURE 9.4: AN EXAMPLE OF A DATA PACKET

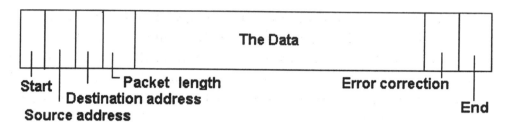

The word processing file that is broken into packets is then rejoined at its destination.

The Need for Speed

An important characteristic of networks is the speed at which the data can travel over the network. If network performance is too slow, employees suffer productivity losses. With too fast a response (this isn't a common problem), companies have overspent on hardware. Speed is correlated with bandwidth, which is how big the pipe is. Bandwidth was fully discussed in Technology 3.

Redundancy

A critical component of network design is redundancy. Redundancy should be designed in at every step. If a server goes down, an entire department can be temporarily crippled. If a server goes down and the load can be switched to another server, productivity does not have to suffer. It's good to have redundant servers, redundant hard drives, and redundant routers. The more that's redundant, the more you have on reserve to keep the network functions running. You can decide how much to spend on redundancy by comparing the cost of redundancy with the cost of downtime.

Many networks employ RAID (redundant arrays of independent disks) storage devices to provide varying levels of data and disk redundancy. For example, some RAID devices mirror, or copy, data on a network so that if a file or a portion of a disk becomes corrupted, it can easily be replaced with another copy. Considerations for choosing a RAID product include capacity, prices, reliability, and compatibility. Compaq, Digital Equipment Corporation (Storage Works line), and Hewlett-Packard are examples of RAID vendors.[3]

RAID's storage system classification was recently simplified to three levels by the RAID Advisory Board: Failure Resistant Disk Systems, Failure Tolerant Disk Systems, and Disaster Tolerant Disk Systems. A plus sign following any of the levels indicates additional features.[4]

File Access

What if both Susan and Bill need to edit the Smith spreadsheet, and they try to open it at the same time? What if they both open the file and edit it? Bill finishes first and saves his file. Susan finishes next and saves her file. When Susan saves her file, Bill loses his work because Susan didn't start with Bill's updated file; she started with the previous generation.

Now that we have more than one person grabbing for files, software on the network must handle resource conflicts such as Susan's and Bill's. With some software, if Bill is faster than Susan, Bill will get the file and Susan will get a message that says someone else has the file. Susan will have to wait until Bill finishes editing the file. This is called file-locking. Susan is locked out of the whole file until Bill is finished.

Other software allows for record-locking. In this case, Susan and Bill can both enter records into a database at the same time. If Susan and Bill try to edit the same record at the same time, the network will manage the conflict by locking one out at the record level, but not out of the entire database.

When buying software for network applications, an important consideration is how resource conflicts are managed. Software will allow for either file-locking or record-locking. Most software salesmen do not understand the difference. CPAs who run across this problem should ask enough questions to find out if the software meets their requirements.

Peer-to-Peer

Some small firms will find that a simpler form of network, called a peer-to-peer network, will be most effective for their needs. In this type of network, there is generally no dedicated server machine and there is no need for a network operating system. A peer-to-peer network will still be cabled and each PC will need a network card. The big difference in peer-to-peer systems is that each user can see files on the other users' computers. This is in contrast to a LAN, where client computers can see LAN drives, but not each other's local hard drives.

You can set up a simple peer-to-peer network using Windows 95 clients. You can also use Artisoft, Inc.'s LANtastic or another peer-to-peer product to set up such a system.

■ ■ ■

Management and Administrative Issues of Networking

Network Expertise

A few years ago, a CPA came to me nearly crying about the overtime hours he was working. His firm of twenty people had just networked their computers, and my friend was picked to manage the network. He was

Figure 9.5: An Example of a Peer-to-Peer Network

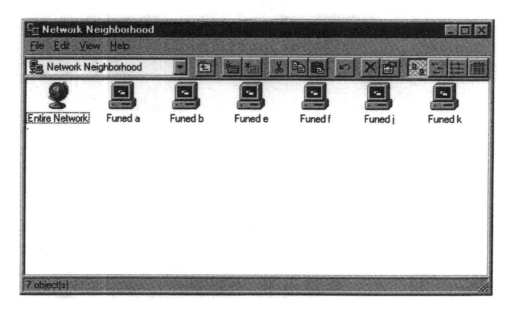

Figure 9.6: Artisoft, Inc.'s LANtastic is a Popular Peer-to-Peer Product

selected because he was their most computer-literate employee. This new network manager was expected to keep up with his old duties in addition to his new duties. He was even expected to generate the same level of billable hours while managing the network. Would you say that's a little unrealistic today? It didn't take my friend long to find another job. His old firm was "up a creek" when my friend left because of the firm's excessive expectations.

The job of network administration is a large one. Approximately one staff person should be hired for every fifty PCs on the network. Complexities such as remote access, Internet access, and network security can drive the staff level higher. Most companies with tight budgets will try to squeeze by with one network person per one hundred clients.

The primary tasks of a network administrator are—

- Keeping the network up and running.
- Controlling user access through ID maintenance.

- Monitoring and planning for network resources, such as throughput, traffic, memory, and storage.

- Overseeing the backup function.

- Planning for and installing hardware, cable, and software upgrades.

- Preparing and testing a disaster-recovery plan.

- Fielding software and hardware questions from end-users. If the company does not have a separate help desk function or end-user computing department, the network administrator is often absorbed into the duties of answering software questions and troubleshooting users' PCs.

Asset Management

There's a lot of money invested in building a network. Network management policies must be written to manage these large-dollar assets. The policy should address the following:

1. *Asset purchase.* What must be cost-justified through the capital approval process? Will acquisitions be centralized? Has leasing been considered as an option? Who will be responsible for installation?

2. *Asset standards.* What types of PC should be purchased? Sticking with a minimum number of vendors and configurations is cheaper and reduces complexity. Standardize on no more than three variations of workstations. Keep everyone on the same release of software. Adhering to standards will reduce training and support costs as well as network complexity.

3. *Inventory tracking.* Who will track PCs physically? While I was an information systems manager at a Fortune 500 company, a system unit in the training lab disappeared. We noticed it immediately, but we might not have noticed it if it disappeared out of a cubicle that was not currently staffed. What about tracking software, including manuals and diskettes or CD-ROMs? Who will monitor software license compliance? Although we learned in Technology 1 that many people do not pay for their software, many large companies are over-licensed by 12 percent.[5]

4. *Asset maintenance.* What happens when a PC breaks or a user has a question? Do you have the necessary support function in place? Is the network administrator answering desktop questions about Microsoft Excel, and if so, is that a good use of his or her time? Or can a lower-paid help desk employee field some of the desktop questions from users? Is the money that is spent on these functions tracked and budgeted?

5. *Asset upgrades.* Do you have an automated system to distribute software upgrades? Or do you have the installation files stored on a LAN drive so that users can perform the installs themselves?

6. *Asset disposal.* How is the equipment disposed of? Will it be sold for parts or donated to a nonprofit group?

7. *Asset reporting.* Does the accounting department have the necessary information for the proper recording of assets on its balance sheet?

Companies that have network asset management policies in place can save big, anywhere from 13 percent to 26 percent, according to two surveys on the subject.[6]

■ ■ ■
Trends in Network Operating Systems

It's a two-horse race in the battle among network operating systems. Although Novell's NetWare has a large, loyal, installed base, especially among CPAs, the relatively new Microsoft Windows NT Server is fast gaining market share. Figure 9.7 presents the percentage of installed

Figure 9.7: Network Operating Systems in Use as of Mid-1996

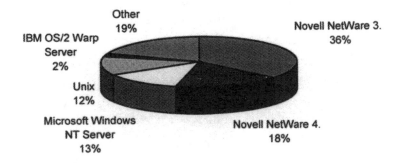

Other
19%

IBM OS/2 Warp
Server
2%

Unix
12%

Microsoft Windows
NT Server
13%

Novell NetWare 3.
36%

Novell NetWare 4.
18%

operating systems, tabulated from a *Computerworld* survey of more than thirty-five hundred users in mid-1996.[7]

A Great File Server or a Great Application Server?

The strengths and weaknesses of Novell's NetWare include—

- Strong file and print services.
- Strong directory service.
- Strong support from third-party vendors in their development of add-on utilities.
- Relative weakness in applications services.

FIGURE 9.8: WEB BROCHURE OF NOVELL'S NETWARE

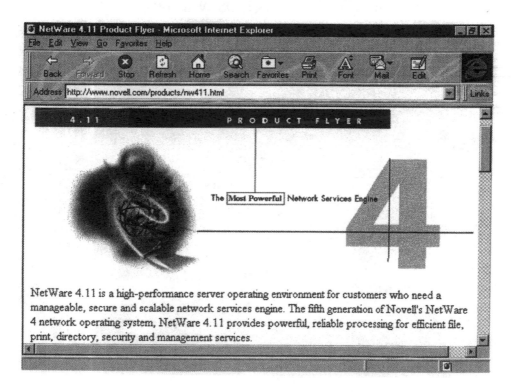

The strengths and weaknesses of Microsoft's Windows NT Server include—

- Strong applications services.
- Relative weakness in file and print services.
- Relative weakness in directory services.
- Somewhat strong remote services (not considering third-party products).[8]

In a nutshell: NetWare is the better choice for large, enterprise-wide networks with more than three servers. Windows NT is better deployed in small companies. Windows NT also works best when installed in tandem with Microsoft's Back Office.

Both NetWare and Windows NT run in conjunction with a variety of client operating systems, such as DOS, Windows 3.*, Windows for Workgroups, Windows 95, Windows NT, MacIntosh, OS/2, and Unix.

FIGURE 9.9: WEB BROCHURE OF MICROSOFT WINDOWS NT SERVER

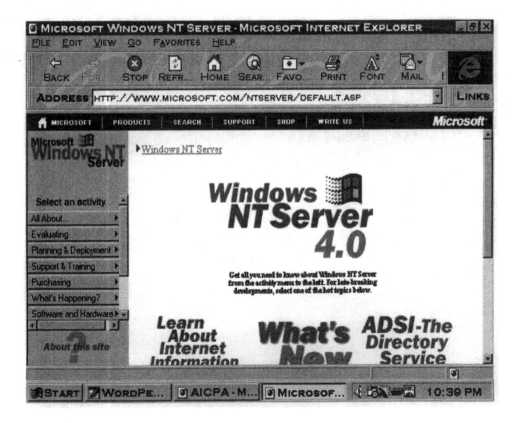

A majority of companies have chosen both network operating systems. Their strategy is to deploy NetWare for enterprise-wide networks and to run Windows NT side by side for application services.

Last but not Least

OS/2 Warp deserves at least a sentence here. Technically, it rates higher than both market leaders NetWare and Windows NT. OS/2 Warp has superior file and print services and better-than-average directory services and applications services. It's also cheaper to run than either NetWare or NT. Unfortunately, its low market share is a factor in companies' decisions.

INTRANETS

The rage in networking topics this year is intranets, the hottest technology since client/server systems, and businesses are rushing in.

The definition of intranets will vary depending on whom you talk to. Generally, an intranet refers to the use of Internet technologies within a company, such as the use of browsers, search engines, and HTML (hypertext markup language) documents. An intranet does not have to be connected to the Internet.

Benefits and Uses

What makes an intranet so attractive? First, it is really fast to post documents using HTML. HTML is a fast, easy language to learn, and many software tools have been created to convert or attach word processing documents to HTML documents. The types of documents that are getting immediate implementation on an intranet include—

- Company telephone directories.
- Company and department policies and procedures.
- Catalogs and price lists.
- Human resource department announcements.
- Corporate press releases.
- Job openings.

As you can see, documents with large distributions are good candidates for intranet page content. The company saves printing expense, postage, and distribution labor. The employee can access the documents with browser software that is on his or her desktop. Some of the more popular browsers include Netscape Navigator and Microsoft Internet Explorer.

One great benefit of using browsers is that they are platform-independent. You can put them on an Apple, a PC, or a Unix box. Browsers are also cheap. Microsoft gives Internet Explorer away free.

Posting internal documents is the number one use of intranets. Other uses include—

- Groupware to develop products and services.
- Group document review.
- Email, using SMTP (Simple Mail Transfer Protocol).[9]
- Collaboration.
- Discussions.
- Line-of-business applications.
- Links to partners and customers.
- Electronic commerce.[10]

Most companies using intranets are seeing tremendous savings in printing, distribution, and mailing costs. Other savings will depend on what the intranet is used for. For example, one company is saving training costs by distributing training materials on the intranet.

Costs and Surprises

The costs of intranets vary, depending on their intended uses. Existing networks with TCP/IP capability, staff, and software can be deployed to build the intranet fairly cheaply. This cheap entry into intranets has caused some firms to bypass cost-justification analyses and rush into intranet projects. A recent *Computerworld* survey showed that sixty-three of one hundred firms did not cost-justify intranets before building them.[11]

Hmmm. Remember when client/server applications first appeared? Remember how cheap we first thought client/server technologies were? Some companies that rushed into client/server systems learned a painful lesson.

An intranet effort should be cost-estimated and cost-justified like any software project. Some of the questions that will help to accurately estimate the intranet budget include the following.

- Do you have TCP/IP capabilities on your network? TCP/IP (transmission control protocol/Internet protocol) is the protocol of Internet technologies. If you are running Windows NT, you are already TCP/IP-enabled. If you are running Novell NetWare, you can install Novell's IntranetWare to add the TCP/IP protocol.

- Will you have to upgrade any hardware?

- What will intranet use do to your existing bandwidth capabilities?

- Who will develop and maintain the content?

- Who will maintain the new program libraries?

- Who will coordinate user administration and other intranet administration tasks?

- What business applications do you wish to link with the intranet and what will the interfaces cost?

- Will you connect to the Internet? Which firewall will you implement?

- Will additional intranet tools be purchased?

On the benefit side, consider the following:

1. What are the quantifiable savings? (Look at printing, distribution, mailing, and so forth.)

2. What are the soft savings? (Look at customer service improvements, new ideas, employee productivity, and so forth.)

3. What is the cost of not investing?[12]

Web Tools

Intranet tools are still in the primitive stage, but are blossoming as vendors invest in the fury and popularity of the intranet. It may take a few years to develop the sophistication in intranet tools that is available in other products.

Intranet Management

In large companies, intranets can get out of hand quickly if departments and groups of people decide to install their own without waiting for the systems department. For companies planning more than a few intranets, a centralized function that develops intranet standards will help to organize efforts and make them more effective for all in the company.[13]

The goal of intranets is for employees to find information quickly, and a structure must be developed so that intranets maintain their usefulness. Standards and an organization plan will help to structure the data. Search engines will help employees find data on an intranet with thousands of pages. Designers should include site maps and search options on every page. Training sessions also help some users get around better. An employee who can find data faster is not only productive, but also reduces network traffic.[14]

ELECTRONIC DATA INTERCHANGE

technology 10

Electronic Data Interchange (EDI) is 1997's Technology 10. To that you might say, "Ho hum." After all, EDI has been around for twenty years. Plus, it's only for large companies, right? A few years ago, the answer was "yes." But today, exciting things are happening in EDI. The Internet brings a completely new cost and time picture to EDI. And, more important, EDI is now affordable for small businesses.

EDI is the technology that allows companies to send business transactions to each other in a standard electronic format. Companies that participate in EDI are called *trading partners*. Trading partners send purchase orders, invoices, and many other types of documents back and forth to each other. EDI allows companies to become partially paperless and to reduce data entry costs as transactions move all the way from the originating company's internal processing systems to the receiving company's internal systems.

EDI is an important component of the broader technology of electronic commerce. What distinguishes EDI from other forms of electronic commerce is the fact that EDI transactions are formatted using strict standards that have been agreed to worldwide. Two primary standards exist: X12 and EDIFACT (EDI for Administration, Commerce, and Transport). Other forms of electronic commerce are free-form and do not follow such strict formatting standards.

This chapter presents—

1. The business case for EDI.
2. EDI concepts and terminology.
3. EDI on the Internet.

■ ■ ■
THE BUSINESS CASE FOR EDI

Eighty thousand companies in the United States are using EDI today, estimates Harbinger Corporation, an EDI vendor. But the potential market is much larger, according to Harbinger and another EDI vendor. Harbinger estimates that there are 1.5 million small businesses that would like to communicate with their large-business EDI-enabled customers.[1] General Electric Information Services, Inc. (GEIS), another EDI vendor, puts the number at 1.9 million small to medium-sized businesses.[2]

Why is the number of companies using EDI so small in comparison to the market potential for EDI? The high cost of EDI is the primary reason companies have held back from using EDI. As the costs are driven down, more companies will implement the technology. The Internet will be a major factor in driving costs down by providing a cheaper method of implementation.

Costs

The cost components of EDI include—

- The cost of translation software that is needed to convert the transaction from the company's internal format to a standard EDI format. There are several components to this cost:
  - The prices of translation software packages vary significantly. On average, translation software costs $3,000 to $5,000, according to an analyst at Giga Information Group.[3] For a large company implementing many different types of EDI transactions, the software can cost as much as $50,000.[4] Some EDI vendors give the software away free if you sign up for their monthly value-added-network (VAN) services.
  - Software maintenance contracts are available and advisable. As standards change periodically, the translation software requires updating for the new standard.
  - Any additional cost for internal software programming relating to translation should be included in your EDI budget along with the translation software package price.
- Hardware costs. If additional hardware is required to support EDI, these costs should be included.
- The method of transport for the transaction, which is some type of network. The two most common solutions are—
  - A value-added network (VAN). Costs for a VAN include the cost of a mailbox and costs per transaction. For small businesses, the monthly tab can be as little as $100 to $400 per month.[5] A large company with 125,000 transactions per month can spend $50,000 to $100,000. Some companies offer a 20 percent discount if the transactions can be sent during off-peak hours.[6]
  - The Internet. The cost of sending EDI transactions over the Internet is one-third to one-fifth the cost of using a VAN.

- The legal costs of setting up contracts between the company and its trading partners and between the company and a VAN.

- Training costs for EDI staff.

- Any consulting services needed during system setup.

- Staff costs of monitoring the system (or the VAN) and soliciting new trading partners.

Benefits

The results of a survey asking more than one thousand firms why they use EDI are shown in table 10.1.[7]

EDI is a giant step for firms wishing to implement the paperless office. EDI transactions flow seamlessly from one company's internal systems to another company's systems. The transaction—let's say a purchase order—is entered into the originating company's systems. Software translates it to EDI format, it is sent over the network, and the receiving company accepts it into its systems. The receiving company translates the purchase order from EDI format to a format that its order entry system can understand. The company is well on its way to processing the order. This not only precludes paper handling, but it also precludes the step of data entry for the receiving company. Data entry labor is reduced, and so is the potential for errors.

New Balance Athletic Shoe, Inc. is one company trying to outstep its competition with EDI. Stores such as Foot Locker and Athlete's Foot can

TABLE 10.1: REASONS GIVEN FOR USING EDI

Advantage	Respondents (%)
Quick response and access to information	47.1
Cost efficiency	20.4
Customer's request	19.2
Effect of EDI on paperwork	12.4
Accuracy	9.8
Better communications	5.7
Ease of processing for order entry	5.5
Aids in accounting and billing	5.5
Better customer service	5.5
Tracing shipments	4.9
Remain competitive	4.9
Industry standards	4.0
Convenience	4.0
Reduction staff	3.7
Reduction in inventory	3.2

send the shoe company EDI-based orders for a particular type of shoe. New Balance can respond faster to consumer demand and rush the shoes to the stores. This leads to a direct increase in sales. 1997's sales are projected to outpace 1996's by 25 percent to 30 percent.[8]

A high-tech firm, Avex Electronics, uses EDI because it frees up its purchasing managers from the clerical part of purchasing. Managers can spend time on strategic issues, such as pricing and negotiations.[9]

Types of Companies Using EDI

The first companies that signed up for EDI included companies in the transportation, drug, food and grocery, and railroad industries.[10]

Besides large companies, other companies that stand to gain big from EDI include—

- Companies that are dependent on future ordering, such as New Balance.[11] EDI cuts cycle time from manufacturing to delivery, thus reducing related inventory expenses. When the turnaround time for ordering products is decreased, a larger number of smaller orders can be placed, matching demand in a just-in-time fashion. Smaller quantities can be ordered, thereby reducing the risk of being stuck with a large volume of items that do not sell well.

- Certain industries, such as health care. Some hospitals are looking to build links with insurance providers.[12] An EDI system can pay for itself quickly by automating the paperwork shuffle in this industry.

- Companies that sell to the U.S. government. The U.S. government feels so strongly about EDI that it offers training and consulting for its suppliers as an encouragement to implement it.[13]

- Small businesses that are being targeted by new Internet/EDI products and services. For example, last year GEIS announced TradeWeb, a service that has an annual fee of about $1,000.[14] Companies that send a small number of transactions per month can consider a service like TradeWeb.

A few large companies that are heavily invested in EDI expect others that do business with them to use EDI as well. The large company saves money when everyone it does business with is EDI-compliant. Wal-Mart is one company that has implemented a strict EDI policy: it will not do business with a firm that cannot implement EDI.

■ ■ ■ EDI CONCEPTS AND TERMINOLOGY

EDI allows businesses, called trading partners, to transact business electronically. The transactions are sent from trading partner to trading partner via a network. The layout of the transactions, or documents, follow a specific format that is set by a standards body. Each of these components is discussed in detail in the remainder of this chapter.

Trading Partners

First of all, EDI cannot be done "on the fly." Two companies must agree to become trading partners. They usually execute a trading partner agreement, which is a legally binding contract that spells out how the EDI transactions will be handled as well as what the trade terms and conditions will be between the two companies.[15]

Companies that are good candidates for trading partners are companies that already have good business relationships with each other. Becoming a trading partner requires an even closer relationship with a company. Companies that are trading partners are dependent on one another to process transactions and deliver on them in a timely and accurate manner. The issue of dependency should be considered when selecting trading partners. A chain of trading partners is only as strong as its weakest link. Senior management should be closely involved in soliciting and selecting trading partners.

To fully take advantage of EDI, the number of trading partners should grow year after year. Some companies campaign hard for trading partners and actively solicit them through trade organization meetings and conventions. Some organizations have even presented awards for companies that solicit the largest number of trading partners in any one year. Companies should not underestimate the amount of time it takes to solicit and maintain trading partner relationships.

Types of Documents or Transactions

Companies conduct hundreds of different types of transactions with each other in the normal course of business. All of these transaction types must be considered and defined in the EDI standards. The most common types of transactions that EDI is used for, according to one survey, are shown in figure 10.1.[16]

FIGURE 10.1: TYPES OF EDI DOCUMENTS

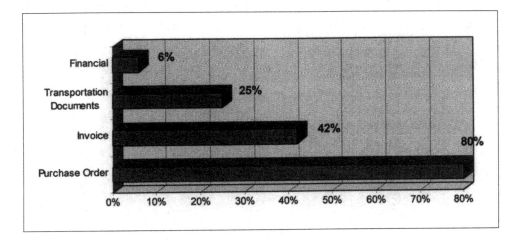

In figure 10.1's terminology, transportation documents include shipping documents, and financial transactions include electronic payments.

Standards

A critical requirement of EDI is the strict formatting standards EDI transactions must follow. An electronic transaction is not considered an EDI transaction unless it observes one of the following two globally accepted standards:

1. *X12.* Companies in the United States widely use the X12 formats, which were designed by the Accredited Standards Committee (ASC) that was chartered by the American National Standards Institute (ANSI). The X12 standards have evolved over several years and are mature.

2. *EDIFACT (EDI for Administration, Commerce, and Transport).* This standard, created by the United Nations, is widely accepted in Europe and other parts of the world. Eventually it will become the only existing standard, which is ideal for everyone. The EDIFACT standards are not as mature as the X12 standards, but are catching up fast. Companies using X12 will eventually have to convert to the EDIFACT standard.[17]

The standards define every transaction type imaginable. When I searched for *Purchase Order* on the DISA (Data Interchange Standards Association) Web site, I got nineteen matches, including Vehicle Shipping Order, Real Estate Title Insurance Services Order, Delivery/Pickup Order, U.S. Customs Carrier General Order Status, Maintenance Service Order, Grocery Products Purchase Order Change, and, oh yeah, plain old Purchase Order. The standards provide a comprehensive list of transaction types so that businesses that wish to implement EDI can meet their specific needs.

In addition to defining the many transaction types, the standards define every piece of information (data element or field) that should be included in each transaction type. The layout for each of the fields in each of the transaction types is described by the standard.

The standards are constantly evolving. The X12 standard is being merged into the EDIFACT standard. Changes are issued periodically, causing multiple versions of layouts at any one point in time. An EDI system has

FIGURE 10.2: WEB SITE OF DISA (DATA INTERCHANGE STANDARDS ASSOCIATION)

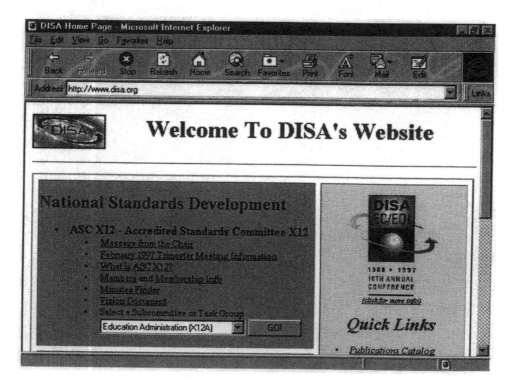

to handle the relevant transaction types and the relevant versions for its trading partners.

EDI Implementation Options

Hardware

Companies use a mix of platforms for EDI systems. Generally, companies transfer transactions from the originating systems, such as purchasing, ordering, or accounts payable systems, to a separate platform for EDI translation. In a survey that was conducted from 1988 to 1991, we can see that EDI translation can be done on just about any type of hardware a company wants to support (see figure 10.3).[18]

FIGURE 10.3: EDI HARDWARE PLATFORMS

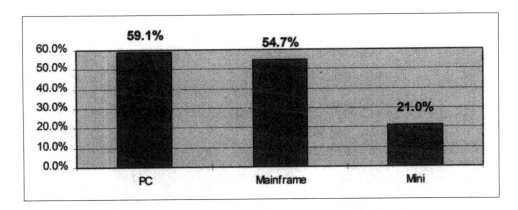

Software

Companies need software that will translate the EDI documents from their internal format to the EDI standard format. Assume a portion of a purchase order looks like figure 10.4 in a company's purchasing system:

FIGURE 10.4: EXAMPLE PURCHASE ORDER LAYOUT FOR A COMPANY

Dept. (4)		Item (10)		Date (8)	
	Customer (6)		Price (10)		...

The numbers in parentheses are field lengths. Now assume that the EDI requirement looks like figure 10.5.

FIGURE 10.5: EXAMPLE EDI LAYOUT

Trading partner 1 (20)	Trading partner 2 (20)	Transaction Type (10)	Date (8)	UPC (20)	Quantity (10)	...

The job of the EDI translation software is to convert the transactions from one format to the other.

Actually, an EDI electronic envelope is quite a bit more complicated than the layout in figure 10.5. EDI transactions are typically batched together with an elaborate set of headers and footers. The X12 envelope includes a communications transport protocol, an interchange control header, a functional group header, a transaction set header, the data, and a trailer for each of the headers mentioned.

The person who maps the data from the company's terminology to the standards body's terminology must understand the definitions in both languages: the company's and the standards'. It's no small undertaking. The mapping has to be done multiple times: once at setup, again whenever the standards change, and again whenever the company changes internal systems.

An example of translation software is Mercator, made by TSI International Software Ltd. in Wilton, Connecticut. Although TSI does not offer VAN services, most VANs offer EDI translation software. That leads us into our discussion of VANs.

VANs (Value Added Networks)

VANs (value-added networks) are the companies that provide private networks that transport EDI transactions from one company to another. Although VANs provide several services, primarily they offer a safe, accurate method of transport for companies' EDI transactions.

VANs handle the security issues of EDI transactions. They make sure EDI transactions arrive safely, and their security software authenticates the EDI transaction. Acknowledgment messages are sent to the originating company notifying the company of successful receipt. VANs can handle the large variety of EDI transactions from a large number of companies and can ensure that transactions are routed to the correct application systems.

VANs also provide trained staff for services and troubleshooting. If a systems problem arises, VANs can help to recover data. VANs can keep a record of EDI transactions for a number of months or years. This archival record is an added service and can be used to resolve disputes between customers and suppliers. Some VANs even help solicit trading partners, and others provide training classes on the technology.[19]

A company wishing to do business with a VAN should execute a third-party network agreement, which is a binding contract between the company and the VAN.[20] The questions a company should ask when deciding on a VAN include—[21]

- What type of hardware and software are supported?
- What type of communications (bandwidth) are supported?
- What mailbox facilities are available?
- What security features are supported?
- What mapping services are supported?
- Will the VAN support current and future EDI standards? How long does it take the VAN to develop the software once a standard is adopted or changed?
- What archiving services are available?
- What redundancy does the VAN have in its system for disaster recovery?
- What response times can you expect? Most companies batch the transactions and run them at night. There is usually a discount for off-hours transmissions. But this also means that it could take from a few hours to a few days to receive an acknowledgment of a transaction.
- Your company will want to audit the VAN. What provisions will be made to perform the audit?

A few of the companies that perform VAN services include—

- General Electric Information Services, Inc., (GEIS)
- IBM's Advantis group
- Premenos Technology Corporation
- Harbinger Corporation
- Sterling Commerce Inc.
- AT&T EasyLink Services

Service Bureaus

One more implementation option for companies that wish to implement EDI but find the price tag too steep is a service bureau. These companies provide a mailbox, receive EDI transactions from a VAN, and forward them to the small companies. New Paradigm-Golden Link is an example of such a company.[22]

FIGURE 10.6: THE WEB PAGE FOR IBM'S ADVANTIS EDI SERVICES

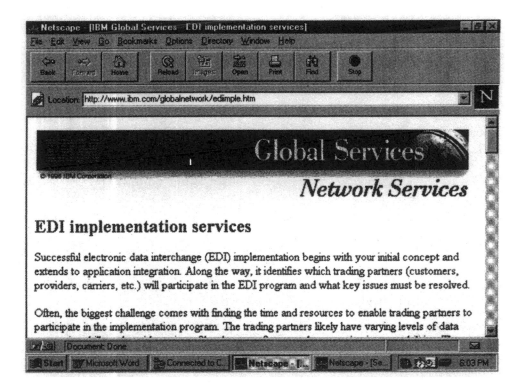

Security

Security is a big issue for companies relying on EDI. Some of the controls that should be considered in an EDI system include—[23]

- *Integrity of the message sequence.* The EDI system should be able to identify records that are out of sequence, duplicated, or missing.

- *Integrity of the message content.* The receiver of the message must be able to determine that the content is original to its sender and has not been modified.

- *Confidentiality.* Messages must be unavailable for anyone other than the intended recipient. No one should be able to read them in transit.

- *Authentication of the originator.* The message must be from the company it says it's from.

- *Receipt authentication.* The message must have been received by its intended recipient.

- *Timeliness.* Messages must be received in a current time frame.

Technology such as encryption is used to provide the necessary security for EDI transactions. You may also see the term MAC or MACing. This stands for Message Authentication Code and refers to transaction authentication using encryption and error-correction technology.[24]

■ ■ ■

EDI ON THE INTERNET

A small but growing percentage of companies employing EDI are using the Internet as their network for EDI transactions. According to a Business Research Group study of three hundred and one companies, 9 percent are using the Internet for EDI transactions.[25] Seven percent of thirty large companies surveyed by Forrester Research Inc. said they were currently testing Internet-based EDI. More than half of the thirty companies said they planned to use the Internet for EDI.[26]

Effectively, companies that choose to implement EDI over the Internet would no longer require the transport services of a VAN. The Internet offers several attractive advantages for companies.

1. *Lower cost.* A VAN charges by volume. The more transactions a company sends, the higher its monthly VAN

bill. Internet usage is generally billed as a flat fee by an Internet service provider. Or, if a company is directly connected to the Internet, it is already absorbing the cost of the leased lines in its network costs. The incremental cost of sending EDI transactions over the Internet is minimal if a company is already connected.

2. *Faster response.* A VAN batches transactions and sends them at night. It takes from several hours to a few days to receive a confirmation of message receipt. A company using the Internet will send transactions as they occur. Receipt occurs in seven to ten minutes.[27]

3. *More potential players.* More companies have access to the Internet. Because it's so affordable, small companies will be able to participate. That further extends the number of businesses that can be connected, which further extends the benefits of EDI to all of the participants.

Some companies believe that the disadvantages of EDI on the Internet are too great at the moment to switch from their comfortable position with their VAN. The primary disadvantage is the lack of security. Sears, Roebuck & Company, for example, is not planning to switch any time soon. Twenty percent of companies surveyed by Forrester Research do not plan to switch to the Internet and like working with VANs.[28]

Those that decide to try the Internet will soon be able to choose from many packaged software applications designed to ease the installation. For example, Premenos offers Templar, a software package that addresses the security issues, including authentication, reliability, receipt notification, and disaster recovery. It runs on Microsoft Windows NT and sells for about $450.[29]

■ ■ ■
SUMMARY

Many companies, especially small businesses, are taking a fresh look at EDI. Although EDI is an old technology, the new technology of the Internet is providing new possibilities for companies looking for an EDI solution.

APPENDIX A:
THE RANKING PROCESS

Now that the top ten technologies have been presented, you might be asking, "Who decided on these technologies?" or "How were the technologies ranked?" We'll answer these questions in this appendix.

■ ■ ■
THE RANKING PROCESS

Late last year, a group of CPAs who are recognized in the profession as technology leaders met, under the sponsorship of the AICPA Information Technology Research and Practices Subcommittees, for one day to produce a list of the technologies that would most affect the CPA profession. The group members used a little bit of advanced technology in the form of a group decision support system (GDSS), which allows participants to interact through networked computers. They met at the University of Arizona campus in the GDSS lab to discuss, list, and rank the technologies, and to answer questions about the profession and about technology in general. The CPAs each had a workstation where they entered their comments and ballots into the GDSS.

A strict agenda was followed for the day. After a familiarization exercise, a brainstorming session was conducted. Questions such as "What new technologies should we be considering and why?" and "What do you think is the most significant technology-related challenge facing the CPA profession today and what should be done about it?" were posed to the group. The answers to these questions, which were entered into the GDSS system, generated a list of forty-seven technologies.

Assigning Stages

The CPAs assigned stages measuring the use and maturity of the technology. Each technology on the list was assigned a value between one and four, as follows:

1. *Stage One*—New technologies in, or emerging from, research and development, but not yet in significant use commercially

2. *Stage Two*—New technologies that are in the early stages of commercial use

3. *Stage Three*—Technologies that are gaining in commercial use and that are expected to be in widespread use within a few years

4. *Stage Four*—Technologies that are now used extensively

The resulting stage rankings for the top ten technologies are shown in figure A.1.

Ranking the Technologies

To rank the technologies, the group of CPAs considered four functional "filters":

1. *Auditing, accounting, and assurance.* The technology has or will have an effect on CPAs in public practice and academia who focus on accounting and auditing and on internal auditors in industry and government.

FIGURE A.1: STAGES OF THE TOP TEN TECHNOLOGIES

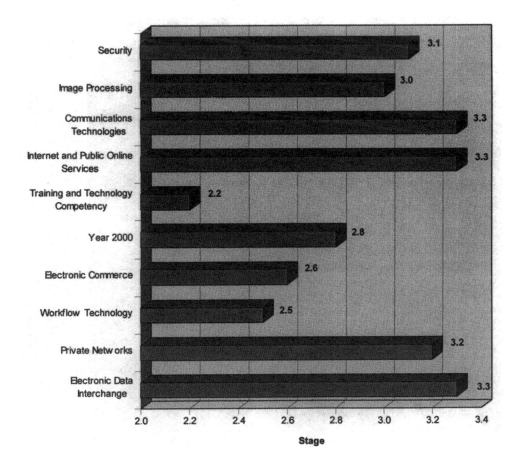

2. *Tax.* The technology has or will have an effect on CPAs in public practice, industry, government, and academia who focus on taxation.

3. *Consulting.* The technology has or will have an effect on CPAs in public practice and in industry and government who focus on providing consulting services to clients or to internal groups.

4. *Financial and Operational Management.* The technology has or will have an effect on CPAs in industry or federal, state, or local government who focus on financial or operational management (for example, controllers, treasurers, business managers, and information systems managers).

A simple one-to-ten, integer-only weighting scheme was used. The guide in table A.1 describes the weights.

TABLE A.1: WEIGHTING SCHEME USED TO RANK TECHNOLOGIES

Weighting Factor		*Effect on Filter*
1.	**Lowest effect**	Technology has little or no effect on the filter.
2–4.	**Some effect**	Technology probably has or will have some effect and information about it might be helpful.
5–6.	**Moderate effect**	Technology has or will have a moderate effect and information about it will be helpful to those affected.
7–9.	**Significant effect**	Technology has or will have a significant effect and should be given some/ medium/ high priority for AICPA members.
10.	**Highest effect (to be used sparingly, not more than 3–5 times for each category of filters)**	Technology has or will have a major effect on the filter and should receive the highest priority for AICPA members.

The following factors were considered by the CPAs when ranking by filters:

1. Impact on revenue
2. Impact on organizational productivity and effectiveness
3. Impact on personal productivity and effectiveness
4. Impact on risks and exposure

From the functional filter ranking, the technologies with the highest means were placed in order. These technologies became the top ten technologies, as shown in table A.2.

The Results

TABLE A.2: RANKING RESULTS

Technology	Accounting, Auditing & Assurance	Tax	Consulting	Financial & Operational Management	Mean
Security	8.07	6.28	7.79	8.69	7.71
Image Processing	7.21	7.55	7.25	7.55	7.39
Communications Technologies	6.86	6.34	7.76	8.07	7.26
Internet & Public Online Services	6.79	6.45	8.10	7.48	7.21
Training & Technology Competency	7.03	6.83	7.34	7.38	7.15
Year 2000	7.21	4.61	8.18	8.36	7.09
Electronic Commerce	7.03	5.10	7.41	7.86	6.85
Workflow Technology	6.59	6.10	7.03	7.62	6.84
Private Networks	6.28	5.55	7.59	7.59	6.75
Electronic Data Interchange	7.03	4.62	7.10	8.07	6.71

Emerging Technologies

The group was also asked to select five emerging technologies—that is, the five technologies most likely to move quickly and have a big impact on CPAs and their clients and employers in the next year. The technologies that received the most votes included—

- Next-generation PC hardware and software.
- Agents.
- Collaborative computing and groupware.
- Smart Cards.
- Telecommuting (tie for fifth place).
- Multimedia (tie for fifth place).

The group continued with two more brainstorming sessions, primarily about what projects the AICPA should focus on in 1997. A debriefing session concluded the day.

Technologies 11 Through 47

The remainder of the technology list is presented in table A.3.

TABLE A.3: TECHNOLOGIES 11 THROUGH 47

11	Telecommuting	30	Mass storage
12	Collaborative computing & groupware	31	Quick response
13	Mail technology	32	Continuous auditing
14	Technology management	33	Data compression & indexing
15	Integrated systems	34	Open hardware architecture
16	Business process reengineering	35	Information on demand (fax on demand)
17	Cooperative & client/server computing	36	Voice systems
18	Management and decision support systems	37	Personal digital assistants
19	Multimedia	38	Societal impacts of computing (privacy)
20	Computer/telephony integration	39	Smart cards
21	Data warehouse	40	PC-cards (network cards)
22	Expert systems	41	Pen-based computing and handwriting recognition
23	Outsourcing	42	Distributed systems management
24	Systems planning & development techniques	43	Digital versatile disk
25	Open software architecture	44	Paperless auditing
26	Next-generation PC hardware & software	45	Machine learning (neural nets)
27	Agents	46	Office equipment integration
28	High-definition video conferencing	47	Global positioning systems
29	Automatic identification technologies (bar coding)		

■ ■ ■

THE TECHNOLOGY

At the University of Arizona, the meeting room was equipped with networked PCs at each workstation. The software used was Ventana's GroupSystemsV electronic meeting software. It captures anonymous text-based messages from a group such as the CPAs and displays the messages as they are entered into the system. In a way, it is like being in an online chat room, only it's a little more organized and the conversation is a little more meaningful (if you've been in a chat room, you'll know what I mean).

The software is great for brainstorming and ranking, as it was used here. It allows for collaboration among individuals. The anonymity factor allows shy people to speak up and prevents talkative individuals from dominating a meeting. Individuals who use this type of technology must be pretty comfortable with technology in general. The tool is a bit overwhelming for the average meeting-goer who is not particularly computer-literate.

■ ■ ■

THE CPAS

The twenty-nine CPAs who ranked this year's list of top ten technologies have an average of more than twenty years of professional experience. Public practice, private industry, education, government, and consulting were represented in the group. Participants work in consulting, auditing, information technology auditing, education, financial management, and information technology management, to name a few.

Each of the CPAs are AICPA members and serve on one of the following AICPA committees:

1. Information Technology Executive Committee
2. Information Technology Research Committee
3. Information Technology Practices Committee
4. Computer Auditing Subcommittee
5. Tax Computer Applications Committee
6. Auditing Standards Board

Everett C. Johnson, Jr. of Deloitte & Touche led the meeting. The names of the voting participants were as follows:

- Ken Askelson, JC Penney Company
- Luther E. Birdzell, Arthur Andersen
- L. Gary Boomer, Boomer Consulting
- Dan Briano, Ross Systems
- Christopher L. Brooks, Cellex-C Distribution
- Janet G. Caswell, Janet Caswell CPA, PC
- Tom Cleveland, Management and Capital Group
- Nancy Cohen, AICPA
- Mark Eckman, AT&T
- Philip Friedlander, Ernst & Young, LLP
- Croley Graham, Lattimore, Black, Morgan, & Cain
- Mike Groomer, Indiana University
- Wayne Harding, Great Plains Software
- Glenn Helms, University of North Carolina
- Roman Kepczyk, Boomer Consulting
- Carol A. Langelier, U.S. General Accounting Office
- Christopher J. Leach, Leach Consulting & Accounting

- Louis Matherne, AICPA

- James C. Metzler, Gaines, Metzler, Kriner & Co., LLP

- Janis R. Monroe, MicroMash

- Belverd E. Needles, Jr., DePaul University

- Ed Odmark, AFC Enterprises

- Mark Payne, KPMG Peat Marwick, LLP

- Gene Prescott, C. Eugene Prescott, CPA

- Rick Richardson, DreanStreet Productions

- Carolyn Sechler, Sechler & Associates, PC

- Sandi Smith, Sandra L. Smith, CPA.

- George W. Wilson, Jr., Turner, Wilson & Co.

- William Zimmerman, French McGowen & Co., PC

All of these individuals volunteered their time for a process like this because they are interested in and dedicated to forwarding and disseminating technological knowledge and awareness in the CPA profession.

APPENDIX B:
FURTHER READING AND RESEARCH

How can we keep up with the crazy pace of technology? This appendix is designed to point you in the right direction if you wish to expand your knowledge of technology topics past the summaries that I have provided in this book.

■ ■ ■

TECHNOLOGY MAGAZINES—HARD COPY AND ONLINE

Although I know we are told we should get away from paper, I find a few magazines irresistible in hard copy format, namely *Computerworld* and *PC World*. There are many acceptable alternatives to these two, such as *Information Week, PC Week,* and *PC Magazine*.

Also, hundreds of specialty technology magazines exist, such as *Communications Week* and *Network Computing*. Subscribing to a magazine that specializes in an area you're interested in is a good way to gain more depth in that area. One way to get to some of that content without subscribing to fifty magazines is to view some of the technology magazine Web sites, such as—

- *C/Net* (http://www.cnet.com), which offers technology items with a news emphasis. Use its search engine in the www.news.com portion of its site for the best hits.

- *TechWeb* (http://www.techweb.com), which offers a great search engine that scans a dozen magazines published by CMP, Inc., including *Communications Week, Information Week,* and *Network Computing*.

- *Computerworld* (http://www.computerworld.com), which has its own site of searchable articles from back issues.

- *Datamation* (http://www.datamation.com), which has full text of articles and information for information systems managers, is another good site.

■ ■ ■

ACCOUNTING MAGAZINES—HARD COPY AND ONLINE

Because accounting magazines print news covering the gamut of professional topics, you can occasionally find technology articles. When you do, they are specific to CPAs, unlike those in the more general technology sources already mentioned. These magazines include *Journal of Accountancy, Accounting Today,* and *Management Accounting.*

Online, the sites worth visiting every once in a while include—

- *Faulkner & Gray* (http://www.electronicaccountant.com).
- *Commerce Clearing House, Inc.* (http://www.cch.com).
- *Harcourt Brace Professional Publishing, Inc.* (http://www.hbpp.com).

■ ■ ■
General Business Magazines—Hard Copy and Online

One great measuring stick is this: if a technology has been reported on in a mainstream publication, it's time to learn more about that technology. My favorite mainstream publications that cover technology include *The Wall Street Journal, Forbes ASAP,* and *Time.* There are many worthy alternatives to these, depending on personal preference, such as *Newsweek* and *Fortune.* Many of these sources have online sites that supplement the paper versions.

■ ■ ■
Other Online Sources

Besides magazine and news sites, many other online sites have valuable information about technology:

1. *Vendors.* Often vendors that sell a technological product post white papers or FAQs (lists of frequently asked questions) to help educate the consumer about that technology.
2. *Professional and Trade Associations.* If the technology is represented by a trade association, that association will likely post white papers or other articles about the technology. The AICPA's Web site (http://www.aicpa.org) is a great example.
3. *Big Six or Competitors.* The Big Six sites contain a wealth of knowledge about lots of accounting and technology topics.

■ ■ ■
Other Sources of Information

Other places to look for information on technology include—

- Training aids, such as books, conferences, courses, and conventions. Refer to the chapter on technology 5 for a more extensive list of training sources.

FIGURE B.1: THE AICPA HOME PAGE

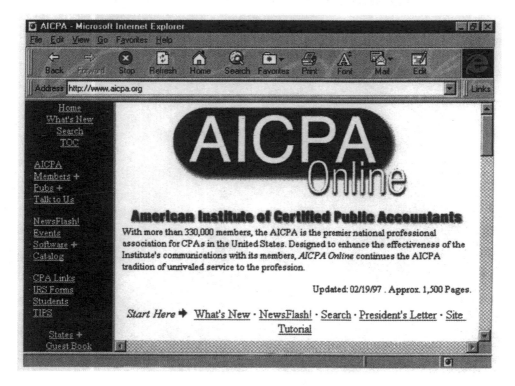

■ Professional association and users' group meetings. The AICPA's Information Technology Membership Section is dedicated to increasing the technological literacy level of CPAs. (See page 249.)

ENDNOTES

TECHNOLOGY 1: SECURITY

[1]"Air Force Web Site Shut as Hackers Gain Access, Change Files", *The Wall Street Journal,* December 31, 1996, page 10.

[2]Philip E. Ross, "Cops Versus Robbers in Cyberspace", *Forbes,* September 9, 1996, page 134.

[3]Gary H. Anthes, "Hack Attack: Cyberthieves Siphon Millions from U. S. Firms", *Computerworld,* April 15, 1996, page 81.

[4]Sewell Chan, "Electronic Vandals Tamper with Web Pages", *The Wall Street Journal,* June 26, 1996, page B1.

[5]Quentin Hardy, "Firms are Hurt by Break-ins at Computers", *The Wall Street Journal,* November 21, 1996, page B4.

[6]"Internet Vulnerability, Malicious Internal Attacks by Employees and Lack of Confidence are Key Findings in Ernst & Young/*Information Week's* 4th Annual Information Security Survey", October 21, 1996, found at http://www.ey.com/us/press/infosec.htm.

[7]Ibid.

[8]Gary H. Anthes and Lisa Picarille, "Viral Threats as Dangerous as Ever", *Computerworld,* August 19, 1996, page 45.

[9]Srikumar S. Rao, "The Hot Zone", *Forbes,* November 18, 1996, page 252.

[10]Gary H. Anthes, "Old, New Viruses Swarm PC Users", *Computerworld,* May 6, 1996, page 55.

[11]Ibid.

[12]Ibid.

[13]Ibid.

[14]Lisa Picarille, "Word Users Cautious as Macro Viruses Multiply", *Computerworld,* August 19, 1996, page 45.

[15]Gary H. Anthes, "Lethal Strain Could Wipe Out Disks this Thursday", *Computerworld,* August 19, 1996, page 45.

[16]Gary H. Anthes, "Hoax Viruses Pose Threat", *Computerworld,* December 9, 1996, page 71.

[17]Srikumar S. Rao, "The Hot Zone", *Forbes,* November 18, 1996, page 252.

[18]Gary H. Anthes, "Hack Attack: Cyberthieves Siphon Millions from U. S. Firms", *Computerworld,* April 15, 1996, page 81.

[19]"Snapshot: Weaknesses in Corporate Information Security Policies, *Computerworld,* April 8, 1996, page 64.

[20]Ibid.

[21]Ibid.

[22]Steve Alexander, "The Long Arm of The Law," *Computerworld,* May 6, 1996, page 99.

[23]Jeffrey Young, "Spies Like Us", *Forbes ASAP,* June 3, 1996, page 71.

[24]Ibid.

[25]Steve Alexander, "The Long Arm of The Law," *Computerworld,* May 6, 1996, page 99.

[26]"Internet Vulnerability, Malicious Internal Attacks by Employees and Lack of Confidence are Key Findings in Ernst & Young/*Information Week's* 4th Annual Information Security Survey", October 21, 1996, found at http://www.ey.com/us/press/infosec.htm.

[27]Jeffrey Young, "Spies Like Us", *Forbes ASAP,* June 3, 1996, page 71.

[28]Kristi Essick, "Symantic CEO Cleared in Trade Secret Case", November 26, 1996, found at http://www.computerworld.com.

[29]Jeffrey Young, "Spies Like Us", *Forbes ASAP,* June 3, 1996, page 71.

[30]Gary H. Anthes, "Distributed Defense", *Computerworld,* December 2, 1996, page 81.

[31]Jeffrey Rothfeder, "No Privacy on the Net", *PC World,* February 1997, page 223.

[32]Sewell Chan, "Electronic Vandals Tamper with Web Pages", *The Wall Street Journal,* June 26, 1996, page B1.

[33]Ibid.

[34]"Air Force Web Site Shut as Hackers Gain Access, Change Files", *The Wall Street Journal,* December 31, 1996, page 10.

[35]Jeffrey Young, "Spies Like Us", *Forbes ASAP,* June 3, 1996, page 71.

[36]Steve Alexander, "The Long Arm of The Law", *Computerworld,* May 6, 1996, page 99.

[37]Gary H. Anthes, "Hack Attack: Cyberthieves Siphon Millions from U. S. Firms", *Computerworld,* April 15, 1996, page 81.

[38]Justin Hibbard, "Solid Plans Keep IS High and Dry", *Computerworld,* January 13, 1997, page 59.

[39]Kelly Jackson Higgins, "The Encryption Prescription", *Communications Week,* December 9, 1996, found at http://www.techweb.com.

[40]Laura Hunt and Mitch Betts, "Alt.cw Index", *Computerworld,* September 23, 1996, page 134.

[41]Gary H. Anthes and Lisa Picarille, "Viral Threats as Dangerous as Ever", *Computerworld,* August 19, 1996, page 45.

[42]Srikumar S. Rao, "The Hot Zone", *Forbes,* November 18, 1996, page 252.

[43]Gary H. Anthes, "SWAT Battles Viruses", *Computerworld,* December 16, 1996, page 87.

[44]Srikumar S. Rao, "The Hot Zone", *Forbes,* November 18, 1996, page 252.

[45]Kelly Jackson Higgins, "The Encryption Prescription", *Communications Week,* December 9, 1996, found at http://www.techweb.com.

[46]Gary H. Anthes, "Push Is On for Safer Standard", *Computerworld,* November 25, 1996, page 65.

[47]Margie Semilof, "Wells Fargo Move Signals Major E-Commerce Advance", *TechWire,* December 18, 1996, found on the Pointcast Network via TechWeb.

[48]Leslie Goff, "Internet Insecurity", *Computerworld,* November 4, 1996, page 121.

[49]Amy Malloy, "How to Choose a Firewall", *Computerworld,* November 4, 1996, page 143.

[50]Patrick Thibodeau, "Security Experts Warn of Christmas Day Hack Attacks", *Computerworld,* December 16, 1996, page 28.

[51]Jeffrey Young, "Spies Like Us", *Forbes ASAP,* June 3, 1996, page 71.

[52]"Internet Vulnerability, Malicious Internal Attacks by Employees and Lack of Confidence are Key Findings in Ernst & Young/*Information Week's* 4th Annual Information Security Survey", October 21, 1996, found at http://www.ey.com/us/press/infosec.htm.

[53]Kim S. Nash, "Copyright Issues Haunt IS on 'Net'", *Computerworld,* January 6, 1997, page 1.

[54]Philip E. Ross, "Cops Versus Robbers in Cyberspace", *Forbes,* September 9, 1996, page 134.

[55]Gary H. Anthes, "Software Pirates' Booty Topped $13B, Study Finds", *Computerworld,* January 6, 1997, page 24.

[56]Kim S. Nash, "Copyright Issues Haunt IS on 'Net'", *Computerworld,* January 6, 1997, page 1.

[57]Mitch Wagner, "Web on Privacy Alert", *Computerworld,* April 29, 1996, page 1.

[58]"The World Wide Web Security FAQ", found at http://www.genome.wi.mit.edu/WWW/faqs/wwwsfl.html.

■ ■ ■

TECHNOLOGY 2: IMAGE PROCESSING

[1]Robert W. Scott, "Imaging Equipment Advice: Don't Be a Cheap CPA", *Accounting Today,* April 22–May 5, 1996, page 24.

[2]Kathy Chin Leong, "Mass Appeal—Once Esoteric and Expensive, Imaging Systems Now Fall Within the Reach of All Users", *Communications Week,* May 20, 1996, found at http://www.techweb.com.

[3]Barb Cole, "Workflow Tied to Document Management", *Computerworld,* January 13, 1997, page 52.

[4]Kathy Chin Leong, "Mass Appeal—Once Esoteric and Expensive, Imaging Systems Now Fall Within the Reach of All Users", *Communications Week*, May 20, 1996, found at http://www.techweb.com.

[5]Ibid.

[6]Stephanie Stahl, "Document Management—Make Documents, Not War—Government Contractor Needs to Store Millions of Pages Electronically", *Information Week,* May 20, 1996, found at http://www.techweb.com.

[7]"Cutting Back the Paper Trail at UNC", found at http://www.keyfile.com.

[8]"Customer Success Story: Budget Rent-a-Car", found at http://ww.filenet.com.

[9]"Two Paths to a Paperless CPA Office", *Franklynn Peterson's CPA Computer Report,* March 1996, page 21.

[10]James K. Watson, Jr., Jeetu Patel, Paul Burina, Bob Puccinelli, and Ninju Bohra, "Doculabs' Enterprise Imaging Benchmark Evaluation", found at http://www.aiim.org/aiim/publications/recentinform/index.html.

[11]Lynn Haber, "The Skinny on Scanners", *Computerworld,* April 15, 1996, page 117.

[12]Harry McCracken", "Scanner Mavens: OCR Packages Save Time, Aggravation", *PC World,* June 1996, page 70.

[13]*Audit Implications of Electronic Document Management, AICPA and CICA,* August 1996.

[14]Jeffrey Gordon Angus and Carla Thornton, "Do-It-Yourself CD-ROMS", *PC World,* January 1996, page 173.

[15]*Audit Implications of Electronic Document Management, AICPA and CICA,* August 1996.

[16]Ibid.

[17]Ibid.

[18]Ibid.

[19]Ibid.

[20]John Fontana, "Saros Readies Workflow Suite", *Communications Week,* January 13, 1997, found at http://www.techweb.com.

[21]William Terdoslavich, "Managing Different Data Types—Text, Digital Documents, Images, Sound Files—All Have to be Managed the Same", *Computer Reseller News,* June 24, 1996, found at http://www.techweb.com.

[22]Kathy Chin Leong, "Mass Appeal—Once Esoteric and Expensive, Imaging Systems Now Fall Within the Reach of All Users", *Communications Week*, May 20, 1996, found at http://www.techweb.com.

[23]Darryl K. Taft, "Imaging Expo Features Vendor Partnerships, Contracts", *Computer Reseller News,* October 14, 1996, found at http://www.techweb.com.

[24]Doug Johnson, "The Evolution of Information Storage", found at http://www.aiim.org/aiim/inform/storage.htm.

[25]Jim Flynn, "Use the Web for Imaging!", *Datamation,* June 1, 1996, found at http://www.datamation.com.

[26]Ibid.

■ ■ ■

TECHNOLOGY 3: COMMUNICATIONS TECHNOLOGIES

[1]James Niccolai, "Allies Line Up for 56k Bit Modem Standards", *Computerworld,* December 16, 1996, found at http://www.computerworld.com.

[2]Mindy Blodgett and Kim Girard, "Excited by 56K Modems? Not So Fast!", *Computerworld,* January 13, 1997, found at http://www.computerworld.com.

[3]Cynthia Morgan and Erik Sherman, "Rrrrrrrriiip into the Web!", *Windows Magazine,* January 1, 1997, found at http://www.techweb.com.

[4]Ibid.

[5]Mary E. Thyfault, "High-Speed Networking—The Battle for Bandwidth", *Information Week,* June 10, 1996, found at http://www.techweb.com.

[6]Ron Cates, "Broadband POTS Opens Up New Vistas", *Electronic Engineering Times,* September 16, 1996, found at http://www.techweb.com.

[7]Mary E. Thyfault and Beth Davis, "Bandwidth Boom", *Information Week,* January 6, 1997, found at http://www.techweb.com.

[8]Mary E. Thyfault with Hakhi Alakhum El, "High-Speed Local Access Nears Rollout—MFS Seeks to Get Jump on Bells", *Information Week,* December 16, 1996, found at http://www.techweb.com.

[9]Stephan Ohr, "Net Access to Home Vies for Bandwidth", *Electrical Engineering Times,* December 2, 1996, found at http://www.techweb.com.

[10]Ibid.

[11]Mary E. Thyfault and Beth Davis, "Bandwidth Boom", *Information Week,* January 6, 1997, found at http://www.techweb.com.

[12]Ibid.

[13]Tim Haight, "DirecPC Delivers Really Fast Downloads via Satellite", *NetGuide,* December 1, 1996, found at http://www.techweb.com.

[14]Steve Alexander, "Riding the Frame-Relay Wave", *Computerworld,* November 25, 1996, page 99.

[15]Ibid.

[16]Kim Girard, "MCI Offers Faster Frame Relay", *Computerworld,* December 16, 1996, page 8.

[17]Bob Wallace, "Start-up Cooks Up ATM Over Microwave", *Computerworld,* January 6, 1997, page 6.

[18]Monua Janah, "Bandwidth Boom", *Information Week,* January 6, 1997, found at http://www.techweb.com.

[19]Mindy Blodgett, "Reeling From Remote", *Computerworld,* March 18, 1996, page 51.

[20]Ibid.

[21]Suzanne Hildreth, "Trimming Telecommuting's Price Tag", *Computerworld,* April 8, 1996, page 100.

[22]Ibid.

[23]Mindy Blodgett, "Reeling From Remote", *Computerworld,* March 18, 1996, page 51.

[24]Ibid.

[25]Wayne Rash Jr., "Comparative Review—Reach Out and Touch Your PC", *Information Week,* September 23, 1996, found at http://www.techweb.com.

[26]Andrew S. Pawlak, "Remote Node and Remote Control: Like Peanut Butter and Chocolate", *Network Computing,* May 15, 1996, found at http://www.techweb.com.

[27]Wayne Rash Jr., "Comparative Review—Reach Out and Touch Your PC", *Information Week,* September 23, 1996, found at http://www.techweb.com.

[28]Andrew S. Pawlak, "Remote Node and Remote Control: Like Peanut Butter and Chocolate", *Network Computing,* May 15, 1996, found at http://www.techweb.com.

[29]Patrick Marshall, "New LapLink Offers Easy Remote Control and File Transfer", *PC World,* March 1996, page 92.

[30]Matt Hamblen, "Desktop Video Surge Forecast", *Computerworld,* October 14, 1996, page 85.

[31]Ibid.

[32]Kate Evans-Correia, "Internet Phones on Hold", *Computerworld,* December 23, 1996, page 119.

[33]Richard A. Shaffer, "The Latest Gadget: Phonebots", *Forbes,* April 8, 1996, page 112.

[34]Steve Bass, "Meet Wildfire, My 24-hour Administrative Assistant", *PC World,* July 1996, page 86.

[35]Stan Miastkowski, "All-in-One Fax, E-Mail, Voice Mail, and Web Access for Small Business", *PC World,* August 1996, page 94.

[36]Richard A. Shaffer, "The Latest Gadget: Phonebots", *Forbes,* April 8, 1996, page 112.

[37]"Briefs: Unwired", *Computerworld,* January 20, 1997, page 49.

[38]Dean Takahashi, "Road Warrior", *The Wall Street Journal,* November 18, 1996, page R27.

■ ■ ■

Technology 4: The Internet and Public Online Services

[1]Michael Castelluccio, Ed, "Tech Forum: The Internet—Out There Where the Road Disappears", *Management Accountant,* May 1996, page 51.

[2]"Inside Lines", *Computerworld,* September 16, 1996, page 138.

[3]Thomas E. Weber, "Who Uses the Internet?", *The Wall Street Journal,* December 9, 1996, page R6.

[4]Beverly Goodman, "Internet Brings CPAs More Business and Better Communication, CCH Study Finds," *The Electronic Accountant,* found at http://198.80.144.22/eac/index/html/feats/cchfeat.htm.

[5]Beverly Goodman, "Internet Brings CPAs More Business and Better Communication, CCH Study Finds," *The Electronic Accountant,* found at http://198.80.144.22/eac/index/html/feats/cchfeat.htm.

[6]Jared Sandberg, "What Do They Do On-line?" *The Wall Street Journal,* December 9, 1996, page R8.

[7]Michael Kinsley, "The Morality and Metaphysics of Email", *Forbes ASAP,* December 2, 1996, page 113.

[8]Tim Ouellette, "Users Prefer to Stick With the Fax Machine", *Computerworld,* September 2, 1996, page 55.

[9]Michael Kinsley, "The Morality and Metaphysics of Email", *Forbes ASAP,* December 2, 1996, page 113.

[10]Jared Sandberg, "What Do They Do On-line?" *The Wall Street Journal,* December 9, 1996, page R8.

[11]Robert L Scheier, "Baiting the Web", *Computerworld,* July 8, 1996, page 76.

[12]Mitch Wagner, "Microsoft, PointCast Team to 'Push' Web Information to Users", *Computerworld,* December 16, 1996, page 10.

[13]Beverly Goodman, "Internet Brings CPAs More Business and Better Communication, CCH Study Finds," *The Electronic Accountant,* found at http://198.80.144.22/eac/index/html/feats/cchfeat.htm.

[14]Robert L. Scheier, "Baiting the Web", *Computerworld,* July 8, 1996, page 76.

[15]Ibid.

[16]Thomas E. Weber, "Watching the Web," *The Wall Street Journal,* January 3, 1997.

■ ■ ■

TECHNOLOGY 5: TRAINING AND TECHNOLOGICAL COMPETENCY

[1]*AICPA Information Technology Survey,* AICPA, April 1995, page 47.

[2]*Information Technology Competencies in the Accounting Profession: AICPA Implementation Strategies for IFAC International Education Guideline Number 11,* AICPA, 1996.

[3]Ibid, page 4.

[4]Ibid, page 59.

[5]Ibid, page 8.

[6]Marshall B. Romney, J. Owen Cherrington, Eric L. Denna, "Using Information Systems as a Basis for Teaching Accounting", *Journal of Accounting Education,* Volume 14, Number 1, 1996, page 57.

[7]*Information Technology Competencies in the Accounting Profession: AICPA Implementation Strategies for IFAC International Education Guideline Number 11,* AICPA, 1996, page 10.

[8]Ibid, page 7.

[9]*AICPA Information Technology Survey,* AICPA, April 1995, page 12.

[10]*Information Technology Competencies in the Accounting Profession: AICPA Implementation Strategies for IFAC International Education Guideline Number 11,* AICPA, 1996, page 17.

[11]Tom Duffy, "Finding the Multifaceted Trainer," *Computerworld,* February 5, 1996, page 91.

[12]*Information Technology Competencies in the Accounting Profession: AICPA Implementation Strategies for IFAC International Education Guideline Number 11,* AICPA, 1996, page 22.

[13]Ibid, page 78.

[14]Ibid, page 82.

[15]Ibid, page 87.

[16]Ibid, page 26.

[17]Ibid, page 27.

[18]*AICPA Information Technology Survey,* AICPA, April 1995, page 18.

[19]Ibid, page 27.

[20]Candice Harp, "Winging It," *Computerworld,* October 21, 1996, page 107.

[21]Ibid, page 107.

[22]*Information Technology Competencies in the Accounting Profession: AICPA Implementation Strategies for IFAC International Education Guideline Number 11,* AICPA, 1996, page 17.

[23]Candice Harp, "Winging It," *Computerworld,* October 21, 1996, page 107.

[24]Tom Duffy, "Finding the Multifaceted Trainer," *Computerworld,* February 5, 1996, page 91.

[25]Monua Janah, "Can't Find a Good Trainer? Try Harder!," *Computerworld,* November 27, 1995, page 85.

[26]Elliott Masie, "The Next Learning Trend: On-The-Fly," *The MASIE Center,* found at http://wwwmasie.com/onfly.html.

[27]*AICPA Information Technology Survey,* AICPA, April 1995, page 27.

■ ■ ■

Technology 6: The Year 2000

[1]Jeff Jinnett, "Legal Issues Concerning the Year 2000 Millennium Bug", http://www.year2000.com/archive/legalissues.html, page 2. Jeff is with LeBoeuf, Lamb, Greene \ & McRae, LLP.

[2]Ibid, page 2.

[3]Check: http://www.gartner.com/aboutgg/pressrel/pry2000.html.

[4]Lee Gomes, "Why Prepping Mainframes for 2000 Is So Tough", *The Wall Street Journal,* December 9, 1996, page B1.

[5]Vendor Responses, http://www.wa.gov/dis/2000/survey/.

[6]David Baum, "Union Pacific Stays on Track for 2000", *Datamation*'s Web site (http://www.datamation.com/plugin/workbench/yr2000/stories/unionp.htm)

[7]Charles Babcock, "Visa Gets Credit For Early Compliance", *Computerworld*, November 18, 1996, page 79.

[8]Leon Kappelman, "Year 2000 Upgrades: A Small Price to Pay", *Computerworld*, November 25, 1996, page 33.

[9]Thomas Hoffman, "Year 2000 Problem Comes Bundled With Legacy of Potential Litigation", *Computerworld*, October 14, 1996, page 88.

[10]Jeff Jinnett, "Legal Issues Concerning the Year 2000 Millennium Bug", http://www.year2000.com/archive/legalissues.html, page 6.

[11]Ibid, page 5.

[12]Ibid, page 11.

[13]Ibid, page 13–14.

[14]Julia King, " 'Tough Love' Tackles IS Projects", *Computerworld*, June 19, 1995, cover.

[15]"Year 2000 Scoreboard: Tips from Texaco", *Computerworld*, November 4, 1996, page 88.

[16]"Year 2000 Scoreboard: Millennium Price Watch", *Computerworld*, December 9, 1996, page 85.

[17]Representative Stephen Horn, "US Federal Government Year 2000 Survey", a report to the House Committee on Government Reform and Oversight found at http://www.year2000.com/archive/survey.htm, dated July 30, 1996.

[18]Robert L. Scheier, "The Road to 1/1/00", *Computerworld*, December 9, 1996, page 83.

[19]Ibid, page 83.

[20]Christos J. Andritsoyiannis, "The Year 2000 project at BIAMAX S.A.", http://www.year2000.com/archive/biamax.html, August 26, 1996.

[21]Charles Babcock, "Visa Gets Credit For Early Compliance", *Computerworld*, November 18, 1996, page 79.

[22]Gary H. Anthes, "Feds Face Year 2000 Crisis", *Computerworld*, April 22, 1996, page 1.

[23]Kim Girard and Robert L. Scheier, "Telcos Lag on Year 2000, Analysts Warn", *Computerworld*, November 11, 1996, page 8.

[24]Coopers & Lybrand, LLP, "Our Experience: Transition2000", found at http://www.colybrand.com/clc/st/exper.html.

■ ■ ■

TECHNOLOGY 7: ELECTRONIC COMMERCE

[1]John Evan Frook, "Cisco's $1 Billion Web Site", *TechWire*, December 9, 1996, Web page http://192.215.107.71/wire/news/1209cisco.html.

[2]Clinton Wilder and Stephanie Stahl, "Services and Consulting—Commerce Gets Webbed—Electronic Systems and Services Proliferate in a Wide-Open Market", *Information Week,* September 16, 1996, found on http://www.techweb.com.

[3]Richard J. Koreto, "Small Firms Can Do Big Business Online", *Journal of Accountancy,* October 1996, page 79.

[4]Tracey Miller, "E&Y's Ernie Making Inroads on the Internet", *Accounting Today,* December 16, 1996–January 5, 1997, page 64.

[5]For the figures used in the chart, "Future Shopping Mall?", *Computerworld,* December 2, 1996, page 74.

[6]Ben Heskett, "Trickle-down success stories", *C/Net,* December 30, 1996, found on http://www.news.com/News/.

[7]Mohan, "Building the Virtual Mall", *Computerworld,* January 13, 1997, page 75.

[8]"An introduction to ecash", found at http://digicash.support.nl/publish/ecash_intro/ecash_intro.html.

[9]John Evan Frook, "Cisco's $1 Billion Web Site", *TechWire,* December 9, 1996, Web page http://192.215.107.71/wire/news/1209cisco.html.

[10]Ibid.

[11]Hailey Lynne McKeefry, "Net Success Requires New Business Models—Cos. Can Enhance Value to Customers With Web", *Electronic Buyers' News,* September 23, 1996, found at http://www.techweb.com.

[12]Clinton Wilder and Stephanie Stahl, "Services and Consulting—Commerce Gets Webbed—Electronic Systems and Services Proliferate in a Wide-Open Market", *Information Week,* September 16, 1996, found on http://www.techweb.com.

[13]Tim Clark, "AMP Helps the Competition", *C/Net,* September 6, 1996, found at http://www.news.com/News/.

[14]Clinton Wilder, "Electronic Commerce—The Web 'Ads' Up", *Information Week,* August 5, 1996, found at http://www.techweb.com.

[15]"CCH Survey Says Accounting Firms will Move Rapidly to Market, Service Clients Through Web Sites", *CCH Inc.,* July 22, 1996, found at http://www.cch.com/whatsnew/corpnews/finding2.html.

[16]Tracey Miller, "E&Y's Ernie Making Inroads on the Internet", *Accounting Today,* December 16, 1996–January 5, 1997, page 64.

[17]Debra A. Velsmid, "Spinning Off Web Merchandising Tools", *Computerworld,* December 16, 1996, page 127.

[18]Thomas Hoffman and Kim S. Nash, "Couriers Deliver New 'Net Services", *Computerworld,* January 6, 1997, page 2.

[19]"Alt.cw: Digital Frontiers", *Computerworld,* July 29, 1996, page 106.

[20]Rose Aguilar and Tim Clark, " 'Free Trade Zone' Proposed", *C/Net,* December 17, 1996, found at http://www.news.com/News/.

[21]Gary H. Anthes, "Bill Seeks to Ban 'Net Taxes", *Computerworld,* January 13, 1997, page 24.

[22]Mitch Wagner, "News For You", *Computerworld,* December 2, 1996, page 71.

[23]Ibid.

■ ■ ■

TECHNOLOGY 8: WORKFLOW TECHNOLOGY

[1]Emily Kay, "Document Management—Order from Chaos", *Information Week,* May 13, 1996, found at http://www.techweb.com.

[2]Lenny Liebmann, "Managing Workflow—Chart Your Game Plan", *Communications Week,* February 5, 1996, found at http://www.techweb.com.

[3]Emily Kay, "Document Management—Order from Chaos", *Information Week,* May 13, 1996, found at http://www.techweb.com.

[4]Ibid.

[5]Jeffrey Schwartz, "Automating Workflow Apps", *Communications Week,* July 22, 1996, found at http://www.techweb.com.

[6]Randy Barrett, "Workflow Software: The New Medium of Implementation", September 1996, found at http://www.reengineering.com.

[7]Ibid.

[8]Alice LaPlante, "Invitation to Customers: Come into our Database," *Forbes ASAP,* August 28, 1995, page 125.

[9]Ibid.

[10]Garrett Michael Hayes, "Groupware Showdown", *Computerworld,* September 2, 1996, page 73.

[11]Barb Cole, "Exchange Workflow Gets Help from Third Parties", *Computerworld,* December 16, 1996, page 69.

[12]Nancy Cox, "Teaming with Potential: Novell GroupWise 5.0", *Network Computing,* November 15, 1996, found at http://www.techweb.com.

[13]James Watson, Jr., Jeetu Patel, Rich Medina, and Joe Fenner, "Doculabs' 1996 Enterprise Workflow Benchmark Study", found at http://www.aiim.org.

[14]Barb Cole, "Exchange Workflow Gets Help from Third Parties", *Computerworld,* December 16, 1996, page 69.

[15]Cassimir Medford, "Workflow Finally Delivers", *VAR Business,* November 1, 1996, found at http://www.techweb.com.

[16]Lenny Liebmann, "Managing Workflow—Chart Your Game Plan", *Communications Week,* February 5, 1996, found at http://www.techweb.com.

[17]Emily Kay, "Document Management—Order from Chaos", *Information Week,* May 13, 1996, found at http://www.techweb.com.

[18]Ibid.

[19]Randy Barrett, "Workflow Software: The New Medium of Implementation", September 1996, found at http://www.reengineering.com.

■ ■ ■

TECHNOLOGY 9: PRIVATE NETWORKS

[1]W. Kirwin, "TCO: The Emerging Manageable Desktop", November 25, 1996, found at the Web site of the Gartner Group.

[2]Lura DiDio, "The Future of Networking", *Computerworld*, January 13, 1997, page 49.

[3]Kevin Burden, "The RAID", February 17, 1997, found at http://www.computerworld.com.

[4]Tim Ouellette, "RAID Labels Redone", January 8, 1997, found at http://www.computerworld.com.

[5]Jeffrey Ubois, "Tending Computer Assets", *CFO*, June 1996, page 67.

[6]April Jacobs, "Asset Management Can Shave Big Bucks", *Computerworld*, June 24, 1996, page 6.

[7]Laura DiDio, "Novell Users Hedge Bets", *Computerworld*, September 16, 1996, page 1.

[8]Lynda Radosevich, "Change Is Coming", *Computerworld*, November 4, 1996, page 101.

[9]Joseph Maglitta, "Net Gain, Net Pain," *Computerworld Intranets*, June 24, 1996, page 3.

[10]"Briefs: Today's Intranet Applications", *Computerworld*, January 20, 1997, page 57.

[11]Kim S. Nash, "Figuring Dollars, Sense of Intranets", *Computerworld*, May 27, 1996, page 1.

[12]Joseph Maglitta, "Net Gain, Net Pain," *Computerworld Intranets*, June 24, 1996, page 3.

[13]Justin Hibbard, "IS Tries to Keep Insanity Out of Intranets", *Computerworld*, January 20, 1997, page 57.

[14]Kim S. Nash, "Intranets Get 'Pushy' ", *Computerworld*, September 9, 1996, page 1.

■ ■ ■

TECHNOLOGY 10: ELECTRONIC DATA INTERCHANGE

[1]Daniel Lyons, "The Internet Crashes EDI's Party", *VAR Business*, July 15, 1996, found at http://www.techweb.com.

[2]Juan Carlos Perez, "GEIS Launches TradeWeb in Effort to Bring EDI to 'Net", *Computerworld*, June 14, 1996, found at http://www.computerworld.com.

[3]Ibid.

[4]Richard Adhikari, "Electronic Commerce—EDI Heads for the Net", *Information Week*, May 6, 1996, found at http://www.techweb.com.

[5]Juan Carlos Perez, "GEIS Launches TradeWeb in Effort to Bring EDI to 'Net", *Computerworld*, June 14, 1996, found at http://www.computerworld.com.

[6]Richard Adhikari, "Electronic Commerce—EDI Heads for the Net", *Information Week*, May 6, 1996, found at http://www.techweb.com.

[7]S. Chan, M. Govindan, J. Y. Picard, G. S. Takach, and B. Wright, *EDI Control, Management, and Audit Issues*, AICPA, 1995, page 23.

[8]Julehka Dash, "New Balance Sprints to Speed Athletic Shoe Deliveries", *Computerworld,* found at http://www.computerworld.com.

[9]Diane Trommer, "Avex Tightens Up Supply Chain with Net-Based EDI", *Electronic Buyers' News,* January 6, 1997, found at http://www.techweb.com.

[10]S. Chan, M. Govindan, J. Y. Picard, G. S. Takach, and B. Wright, *EDI Control, Management, and Audit Issues*, AICPA, 1995, page 22.

[11]Julehka Dash, "New Balance Sprints to Speed Athletic Shoe Deliveries", *Computerworld,* found at http://www.computerworld.com.

[12]Daniel Lyons, "The Internet Crashes EDI's Party", *VAR Business,* July 15, 1996, found at http://www.techweb.com.

[13]Christine Curtis, "Keep an Eye on EDI, Even If You Are Not in the Fortune 1000", *Communications Week,* December 16, 1996, found at http://www.techweb.com.

[14]Juan Carlos Perez, "GEIS Launches TradeWeb in Effort to Bring EDI to 'Net", *Computerworld,* June 14, 1996, found at http://www.computerworld.com.

[15]S. Chan, M. Govindan, J. Y. Picard, G. S. Takach, and B. Wright, *EDI Control, Management, and Audit Issues*, AICPA, 1995, page 22.

[16]Ibid. page 9.

[17]Ibid. page 7.

[18]Ibid. page 9.

[19]Richard Adhikari, "Electronic Commerce—EDI Heads for the Net", *Information Week,* May 6, 1996, found at http://www.techweb.com.

[20]S. Chan, M. Govindan, J. Y. Picard, G. S. Takach, and B. Wright, *EDI Control, Management, and Audit Issues*, AICPA, 1995, page 84.

[21]Ibid. page 73.

[22]Richard Adhikari, "Electronic Commerce—EDI Heads for the Net", *Information Week,* May 6, 1996, found at http://www.techweb.com.

[23]S. Chan, M. Govindan, J.Y. Picard, G.S. Takach, and B. Wright, *EDI Control, Management, and Audit Issues*, AICPA, 1995, page 44.

[24]Ibid. page 45.

[25]Juan Carlos Perez, "GEIS Launches TradeWeb in Effort to Bring EDI to 'Net", *Computerworld,* June 14, 1996, found at http://www.computerworld.com.

[26]Richard Adhikari, "Electronic Commerce—EDI Heads for the Net", *Computerworld,* May 6, 1996, found at http://www.techweb.com.

[27]Ibid.

[28]Ibid.

[29]Ibid.

GLOSSARY

ADSL (asymmetrical digital subscriber line). A telephone line that handles high-speed data such as Internet access, video conferencing, interactive TV, and video on demand. The line is split asymmetrically so that more bandwidth can be used from the telephone company to the customer (downstream) than from the customer to the telephone company (upstream).

anti-virus software. A program that detects and removes a virus.

ARPANET (advanced research projects agency network). The research network funded by the U.S. Advanced Research Projects Agency (ARPA). The software was developed by Bolt, Beranek and Newman (BBN), and Honeywell 516 minicomputers were the first hardware used as packet switches. ARPANET was launched in 1969 at four sites, including two University of California campuses, the Stanford Research Institute and the University of Utah.

ATM (asynchronous transfer mode). A network technology for both LANs and WANs that supports realtime voice and video as well as data. The topology uses switches that establish a circuit from input to output port and maintain that connection for the duration of the transmission. This connection-oriented technique is similar to the analog telephone system (POTS).

backbone. In communications, the part of a network that handles the major traffic. It employs the highest-speed transmission paths in the network and may also run the longest distance. Smaller networks are attached to the backbone.

bandwidth. The transmission capacity of an electronic line, such as a communications network, computer bus, or computer channel. In this book, it is expressed in bits per second (bps).

bitmap. A binary representation in which a bit or set of bits corresponds to some part of an object, such as an image or font.

boot sector. An area on disk (usually the first sectors in the first disk partition) reserved for the operating system. On start-up, the computer looks in the boot sectors for the operating system, which must be loaded first.

boot sector virus. A virus written into the boot sectors of a floppy disk. If the floppy is booted, it infects the system. For example, the Michelangelo virus, which destroys data on

This Glossary is based on information contained in *Computer Desktop Encyclopedia,* published in CD-ROM format by The Computer Language Company Inc., 5521 State Park Road, P.O. Box 265, Point Pleasant, PA, 18950-0265, email: sales@computerlanguage.com. The Author and Publisher thank The Computer Language Company for its generosity in permitting the use of its materials.

March 6, Michelangelo's birthday, infects a computer if the virus diskette is left in the drive and booted inadvertently when the computer is turned back on.

bps (bits per second). The measurement of the speed of data transfer in a communications system.

bridge. A device that connects two LAN segments together, which may be of similar or dissimilar types, such as Ethernet and Token Ring. Bridges are inserted into a network to improve performance by keeping traffic contained within smaller segments.

brouter. A communications device that provides the functions of a bridge and router. See *bridge* and *router*.

browser. A program that lets you look through a set of data. Examples of Web browsers include Microsoft's Internet Explorer and Netscape's Navigator.

bursty. Refers to data that is transferred or transmitted in short, uneven spurts. LAN traffic is typically bursty.

business process reengineering. Using information technology to improve performance and cut costs. Its main premise, as popularized by the book *Reengineering the Corporation* by Michael Hammer and James Champy, is to examine the goals of an organization and to redesign work and business processes from the ground up rather than to simply automate existing tasks and functions.

cable. A communications option for accessing the Internet that uses the coaxial cable network. Cable can also be the physical material that connects networked PCs. See also *twisted pair* or *coaxial cable*.

CATV (community antenna TV). The original name for cable TV, which used a single antenna at the highest location in the community. Now refers to cable TV.

CBT (computer-based training). Using the computer for training and instruction. CBT programs are called courseware and provide interactive training sessions for all disciplines. It uses graphics extensively.

CD-I (compact disc—interactive). A compact disc format developed by Philips and Sony that holds data, audio, still video, and animated graphics. It provides up to 144 minutes of CD-quality stereo, 9.5 hours of AM-radio-quality stereo, or 19 hours of monophonic audio.

CD-R (compact disc—recordable). A recordable CD-ROM technology using a disc that can be written only once. The drive that writes the CD-R disc is often called a one-off machine and can also be used as a regular CD-ROM reader.

CD-ROM (compact disc—read only memory). A compact disc format used to hold text, graphics, and hi-fi stereo sound.

chat room. An interactive discussion (by keyboard) about a specific topic that is hosted on an online service or the Internet.

client. A workstation or personal computer in a client/server environment.

client/server.   An architecture in which the client (personal computer or workstation) is the requesting machine and the server is the supplying machine, both of which are connected via a LAN (local area network) or WAN (wide area network). Since the early 1990s, client/server has been the buzzword for building applications on LANs in contrast to centralized minis and mainframes with dedicated terminals.

CMOS (complementary metal-oxide semiconductor).   A small, battery-backed memory bank in a personal computer that is used to hold time, date, and system information, such as drive types.

coaxial cable.   A high-capacity cable used in communications and video, commonly called coax. It contains an insulated solid or stranded wire surrounded by a solid or braided metallic shield and wrapped in a plastic cover.

COLD (computer output to laser disc).   Archiving large volumes of transactions on optical media. Data is stored on optical disks instead of in paper reports or on microfilm or microfiche.

Cookies.   A file that contains information (cookies) created by Web sites that is stored on the user's hard disk. It provides a way for the Web server to keep track of a user's patterns and preferences and, with the cooperation of the Web browser, to store them on the user's own hard disk in a cookies file. The cookies contain a range of URLs (addresses) for which they are valid. When the browser encounters those URLs again, it sends those specific cookies to the Web server.

cryptography.   The conversion of data into a secret code for transmission over a public network. The original text, or plaintext, is converted into a coded equivalent called ciphertext via an encryption algorithm. The ciphertext is decoded (decrypted) at the receiving end and turned back into plaintext.

cryptolope.   A cryptography envelope that wraps around software to protect it from copyright violations.

CSMA/CA (carrier sense multiple access/collision avoidance).   The LAN access method used in Token Ring. When a device wants to gain access to the network, it waits for a token from the network. When the token is received, the device can transmit. The token is passed around and around the network.

CSMA/CD (carrier sense multiple access/collision detection).   The LAN access method used in Ethernet. When a device wants to gain access to the network, it checks to see if the network is free. If it is not, it waits a random amount of time before retrying. If the network is free and two devices access the line at exactly the same time, their signals collide. When the collision is detected, they both back off and each waits a random amount of time before retrying.

cyberspace.   Coined by William Gibson in his novel *Neuromancer,* it is a futuristic computer network that people use by plugging their minds into it. The term is now used to refer to the Internet or to the online or digital world in general. See *Internet.*

DARPA (Defense Advanced Research Projects Agency). The name given to the U.S. Advanced Research Projects Agency during the 1980s. It was later renamed ARPA. See *ARPANET.*

DAT (digital audio tape). A magnetic tape technology used for backing up data. DAT uses 4-mm cassettes that look like thick audio cassettes and conform to the DDS (Digital Data Storage) standard. Raw capacities are 2GB for DDS, 4GB for DDS-2, and 12GB for DDS-3. DAT tape libraries hold from a handful up to several thousand cassettes.

dedicated lines. A communications line that is not shared by other users or organizations.

DES (data encryption standard). A secret key cryptography method that uses a 56-bit key. DES is based on an IBM algorithm that was further developed by the U.S. National Security Agency.

digital certificate. The digital equivalent to an ID card in the RSA public key encryption system. Digital certificates are issued by certification organizations such as VeriSign, Inc., Mountain View, CA, after verifying that a public key belongs to a certain owner.

digital signature. An electronic signature that cannot be forged. It is a coded message that accompanies the text message transmitted over a network. Digital signatures typically are implemented using the de facto standard RSA public key cryptography method.

digital watermark. A pattern of bits embedded into a file used to identify the source of illegal copies. For example, if a digital watermark is placed into a master copy of an audio CD, then all copies of that CD are uniquely identified. If a licensee were to manufacture and distribute them in areas outside of its authorized territory, the watermark provides a trace.

disaster recovery. A plan for duplicating computer operations after a catastrophe occurs, such as a fire or earthquake. It includes routine off-site backup as well as a procedure for activating necessary information systems in a new location.

document capture. Creating a film or electronic image of any picture or paper form. It is accomplished by scanning or photographing an object and turning it into a matrix of dots (raster graphics), the meaning of which is unknown to the computer, only to the human viewer. Scanned images of text may be encoded into computer data with page recognition software (OCR).

domain name. The address of an Internet site—for example, *www.aicpa.org.*

DSL (digital subscriber line). A high-speed telephone line that provides access to the Internet.

dumb terminal. A display terminal without processing capability. It is entirely dependent on the main computer for processing.

DVD (digital versatile disc). The next-generation video CD and high-capacity CD-ROM.

ecash. A system of digital money from Amsterdam-based DigiCash. The concept of ecash can be likened to travelers checks, which are purchased from a bank and then spent with merchants who accept them. Customers purchase ecash by downloading "digital coins" from a participating bank into their personal computers. Payment is made by uploading a certain amount of ecash to a participating vendor. The transactions are encrypted to provide the necessary security for online transfer.

EDI (electronic data interchange). The electronic communication of business transactions, such as orders, confirmations, and invoices, between organizations.

EDIFACT (Electronic Data Interchange for Administration, Commerce, and Transport). An International Standards Organization (ISO) standard for EDI that is proposed to supersede X12 standards to become the worldwide standard.

EDM (electronic document management). A system that captures and manages documents within an organization. It's an umbrella term for document imaging, workflow, and text retrieval.

electronic commerce. Doing business online. It includes purchasing products via online services and the Internet as well as EDI, in which one company's computer queries and transmits purchase orders to another company's computer.

email. The transmission of memos and messages over a network. Users can send mail to a single recipient or broadcast it to multiple users.

email address. The format for addressing a message to an Internet user is USER_NAME @ DOMAIN_NAME. For example, the address of the AICPA Information Technology Team is "infotech@aicpa.org".

encrypt. To encode data for security purposes. See *cryptography*.

Ethernet. A LAN developed by Xerox, Digital, and Intel. It is the most widely used LAN access method. Ethernet connects up to 1,024 nodes at 10Mbps over twisted pair, coax, and optical fiber. Ethernet is a shared media LAN. All stations on the segment share the 10Mbps bandwidth. With switched Ethernet, sender and receiver have a full 10Mbps bandwidth. Fast Ethernet (100BaseT) increases transmission speed to 100Mbps.

FDDI (fiber distributed data interface). An ANSI standard token passing network that uses optical fiber cabling and transmits at 100Mbps up to two kilometers.

fiber optic. Communications systems that use optical fibers for transmission. Fiber-optic transmission became widely used in the 1980s when the long-distance carriers created nationwide systems for carrying voice conversations digitally over optical fibers.

file and record locking. A first-come, first-served technique for managing data in a multiuser environment. The first user to access the file or record prevents, or locks out, other users from accessing it. After the file or record is updated, it is unlocked and available.

firewall. A network node set up as a boundary to prevent traffic from one segment to cross over to another. Firewalls are used to improve network traffic as well as for security purposes. A firewall may be implemented in a router or it may be a device specialized for such purposes.

forms software. Workflow software used to create on-screen data entry forms and provide email routing and tracking of the resulting electronic documents.

forum. An information interchange regarding a specific topic or product that is hosted on an online service. It can include the latest news on the subject, a conferencing capability for questions and answers by participants, and files for downloading fixes, demos, and other related material.

fractional T1.   A service that provides less than full T1 capacity. Increments of 64kbps are provided.

frame relay.   A high-speed packet switching protocol used in WANs. It has become popular for LAN-to-LAN connections across remote distances, and services are provided by all the major carriers.

FTP (file transfer protocol/file transfer program).   In a TCP/IP (transmission control protocol/Internet protocol) network, a set of commands used to log onto the network, list directories, and copy files. FTP programs are designed to handle all types of files.

gateway.   A computer that performs protocol conversion between different types of networks or applications. For example, a gateway can convert a TCP/IP packet to a NetWare IPX packet and vice versa.

Gbps (gigabits per second).   One billion bits per second.

Gigabit Ethernet.   An emerging Ethernet technology that raises transmission speed to 1 Gbps. Its ability to integrate into existing Ethernets is a distinct advantage.

Gopher.   A program that searches for file names and resources on the Internet and presents hierarchical menus to the user. As users select options, they are moved to different Gopher servers on the Internet. Where links have been established, Usenet news and other information can be read directly from Gopher. There are more than seven thousand Gopher servers on the Internet.

groupware.   Software designed for use in a network that serves a group of users working on a related project. Groupware is an evolving concept that is more than multiuser software, which allows access to the same data. Groupware provides a mechanism that helps several users coordinate and keep track of an ongoing project.

GUI (graphical user interface).   A graphics-based user interface that incorporates icons, pull-down menus, and a mouse. The GUI has become the standard way users interact with a computer.

hacker.   A person who can break into computer systems.

HDSL (high bit rate Digital Subscriber Line).   A high-speed telephone line that can be used to access the Internet.

HTML (HyperText Markup Language).   The standard document format used on the World Wide Web. HTML defines the page layout, which includes fonts and graphic elements as well as hypertext links to other documents on the Web. Each hypertext link contains the URL, or address, of a Web page that can reside on the very same server or on any server worldwide, hence the "Worldwide" Web.

HTTP (HyperText Transport Protocol).   The communications protocol used to connect to servers on the Web. Its primary function is to establish a connection with a server and transmit HTML pages to the client browser. Addresses of Web sites begin with an "http://" prefix.

hub. A central connecting device in a network that joins communications lines together in a star configuration.

hypertext. A linkage between related text. For example, by selecting a word in a sentence, information about that word is retrieved if it exists, or the next occurrence of the word is found.

ICR (Intelligent Character Recognition). The machine recognition of hand-printed characters as well as machine printing that is difficult to recognize.

IDSL (Integrated Digital Subscriber Lines). A hybrid of DSL and ISDN, IDSL refers to high-speed telephone lines that can provide access to the Internet.

image processing. The online storage, retrieval, and management of electronic images of documents. The main method of capturing images is by scanning paper documents.

intelligent agent. A software routine that waits in the background and performs an action when a specified event occurs. For example, agents could transmit a summary file on the first day of the month or monitor incoming data and alert the user when a certain transaction has arrived.

Internet. The Internet is made up of more than one hundred thousand interconnected networks in over one hundred countries, consisting of commercial, academic and government networks. Originally developed for the military, the Internet became widely used for academic and commercial research. Today, the Internet is being commercialized into a worldwide information highway.

Internet phone. Technology that allows an individual to make a telephone call over the Internet. The sound quality is primitive, at best.

Interoperable. The ability for one system to communicate or work with another.

intranet. An inhouse Web site that serves the employees of the enterprise. Although intranet pages may link to the Internet, an intranet is not a site accessed by the general public.

IPX (Internetwork Packet Exchange). A NetWare communications protocol used to route messages from one node to another. IPX packets include network addresses and can be routed from one network to another.

IRC (internet relay chat). Computer conferencing on the Internet. There are hundreds of IRC channels on every subject conceivable from more than sixty countries. You have to log onto an IRC server. Once logged on, to get a list of active channels, type "/list". To join a channel named #HOTSTUFF, type "/join #hotstuff".

ISDN (Integrated Services Digital Network). An international telecommunications standard for transmitting voice, video and data over digital lines running at 64kbps. The telephone companies commonly use a 64kbps channel for digitized, two-way voice conversations.

ISDN terminal adapter. A device that adapts a computer to a digital ISDN line. Like a modem, it plugs into the serial port of the computer or into an expansion slot. Some terminal adapters use the parallel port for higher speed. The adapter may also include a regular data or fax/modem and switch automatically between analog and digital depending on the type of call.

ISP (Internet service provider). An organization that provides access to the Internet. The smaller ISPs provide service via modem whereas the larger ones also offer ISDN and private line hookups (T1, fractional T1, and so forth). Customers generally are billed a fixed rate per month, but other charges may apply. For a fee, a Web site can be created and maintained on the ISP servers, which allows the smaller organization or individual user to have a presence on the Web. In addition, unique domain names can be used.

jukebox. A storage device for multiple sets of CD-ROMs, tape cartridges, or disk modules. Using carousels, robot arms and other methods, a jukebox physically moves the storage medium from its assigned location to an optical or magnetic station for reading and writing. Access between modules usually takes several seconds.

kbps (kilobits per second). One thousand bits per second.

LAN (local area network). A communications network that serves users within a confined geographical area. It is made up of servers, workstations, a network operating system, and a communications link.

lines of code. The statements and instructions that a programmer writes when creating a program. One line of this "source code" may generate one machine instruction or several depending on the programming language.

magneto-optical disk. A rewritable optical disk that uses the magneto-optical recording technique.

MAN (metropolitan area network). A communications network that covers a geographic area such as a city or suburb. See *LAN* and *WAN*.

MAU (multi-station access unit). A central hub in a Token Ring local area network. See *hub.*

Mbps (megabits per second). One million bits per second.

NC (network computer). A desktop computer that provides Web connectivity to the Internet and intranets. It is designed to download all applications from a server and to store results back on the server. The network computer is similar to a diskless workstation and does not have floppy or hard disk storage. It uses a compact operating system that can be booted from the network and includes a Web browser and a Java Virtual Machine (interpreter) for running Java applications. Network computers may also include slots for smart cards for user login verification.

network. An arrangement of computers that are interconnected. In communications, a network consists of transmission channels interconnecting all client and server stations as well as all supporting hardware and software.

newsgroup. A collection of messages about a particular subject on the Internet.

news reader. An Internet utility that is used to read the messages in a newsgroup.

NIC (Network Interface Card). A printed circuit board that plugs into both clients (personal computers or workstations) and servers and controls the exchange of data between them.

NLM (NetWare Loadable Module).   Software that enhances or provides additional functions in a NetWare 3.x or higher server. Support for database engines, workstations, network protocols, fax, and print servers are examples.

NOS (network operating system).   An operating system that manages network resources. It manages multiple requests (inputs) concurrently and provides the security necessary in a multiuser environment.

OCR (optical character recognition).   The machine recognition of printed characters. OCR systems can recognize many different OCR fonts, as well as typewriter and computer-printed characters. Advanced OCR systems can recognize hand printing.

online banking.   The process of receiving bank transactions and paying bills online.

online services.   Services provided by a company, such as CompuServe, America Online, Microsoft Network, and Prodigy, that allow a computer user to participate in an online community. The community includes news, weather, and shopping as well as information on a host of topics. Most services provide email and access to the Internet.

optical disk.   A direct-access disk written and read by light. CDs, CD-ROMs, and videodiscs are optical disks that are recorded at the time of manufacture and cannot be erased. WORM (Write Once Read Many) disks and CD-R disks are recorded in the user's environment, but cannot be erased.

packet.   A block of data (a frame) used for transmission in LANs and packet switching systems. In Ethernet LANs, the terms *packets* and *frames* are used synonymously.

packet switching.   A networking technology used in WANs that breaks up a message into smaller packets for transmission and switches them to their required destination. Unlike circuit switching, which requires a constant point-to-point circuit to be established, each packet in a packet-switched network contains a destination address. Thus all packets in a single message do not have to travel the same path. They can be dynamically routed over the network as circuits become available or unavailable. The destination computer reassembles the packets back into their proper sequence.

peer-to-peer network.   A communications network that allows all workstations and computers in the network to act as servers to all other users on the network.

Pixel (PIX[picture] ELement).   The smallest element on a video display screen. A screen is broken up into thousands of tiny dots, and a pixel is one or more dots that are treated as a unit. A pixel can be one dot on a monochrome screen, three dots (red, green, and blue) on a color screen, or clusters of these dots.

POTS (plain old telephone service).

public key cryptography.   Using a two-part code made up of private and public components. To encrypt a message, the published public key of the recipient is used. To decrypt the message, the recipient uses the unpublished private key.

push model.   A data distribution model in which the software automatically delivers data to the user based on some criterion, such as news categories or time of day. A push model operates in contrast with a pull model, in which the user specifically asks for something by performing a search or requesting an existing report, video, or other data type.

RAID (redundant array of independent disks).   A category of disk arrays (two or more drives working together) that provide increased performance and various levels of error recovery and fault tolerance. RAID can be implemented in software using standard disk controllers, or it can be designed into the disk controller itself.

raster.   To perform the conversion of vector graphics images, vector fonts, or outline fonts into bitmaps for display or printing. Unless output is printed on a plotter, which uses vectors directly, all non-bitmapped images must be rasterized into bitmaps for display or printing.

remote control.   Used to take control of an unattended desktop personal computer from a remote location as well as to provide instruction and technical support to remote users. Keystrokes are transmitted from and screen updates are transmitted to the remote machine as all processing takes place in the local computer.

remote node.   In a remote node setup, the user is logged onto the network using the phone line as an extension to the network.

router.   A device that routes data packets from one LAN or WAN to another. Routers see the network as network addresses and all the possible paths between them. They read the network address in each transmitted frame and make a decision on how to send it based on the most expedient route (traffic load, line costs, speed, bad lines, and the like).

satellite communications.   A radio relay station in orbit 22,300 miles above the earth's equator. It travels at the same rate of speed as the earth (geosynchronous), so that it appears stationary. It contains many communications channels that receive analog and digital signals from earth stations. All signals are transmitted within a carrier frequency.

scanner.   A device that reads text, images, and bar codes. Text and bar code scanners recognize printed fonts and bar codes and convert them into a digital format. Graphics scanners convert a printed image into a video image (raster graphics) without recognizing the actual content of the text or pictures.

seamless integration.   An addition of a new application, routine, or device that works smoothly with the existing system. It implies that the new feature can be activated and used without problems.

search engine.   There are various Web sites that maintain directory databases of other Web sites, such as Yahoo, Alta Vista, Lycos, InfoSeek, and Excite.

security.   The protection of data against unauthorized access. Programs and data can be secured by issuing identification numbers and passwords to authorized users of a computer.

server.   A computer in a network shared by multiple users.

SET (Secure Electronic Transaction).   A standard protocol from MasterCard and Visa for securing online credit card payments via the Internet.

SHTTP (Secure HyperText Transfer Protocol). A protocol that provides secure transactions over the Web.

smart card. A credit card with a built-in microprocessor and memory used for identification or financial transactions. When inserted into a reader, it transfers data to and from a central computer. It is more secure than a magnetic stripe card and can be programmed to self-destruct if the wrong password is entered too many times. As a financial transaction card, it can store transactions and maintain a bank balance.

SneakerNet. Carrying floppy disks from one machine to another to exchange information, when you don't have a network.

software license. Grants the right to use software, but usually only on one machine. The terms of individual software licenses vary and are legal contracts. Network licenses and concurrent licenses are special types of software licenses.

software piracy. The illegal copying of software for personal or commercial use.

source code. Programming statements and instructions that are written by a programmer. Source code is what a programmer writes, but it is not directly executable by the computer. It must be converted into machine language by compilers, assemblers, or interpreters.

spaghetti code. Program code written without a coherent structure. The logic moves from routine to routine without returning to a base point, making it hard to follow. It implies excessive use of the GOTO instruction, which directs the computer to branch to another part of the program without a guarantee of returning.

spider. Also known as a crawler, ant, robot ("bot"), and intelligent agent, a spider is a program that searches for information on the Web. It is used to locate new documents and new sites by following hypertext links from server to server and indexing information based on search criteria.

SQL (Structured Query Language). Pronounced "see qwill," a language used to interrogate and process data in a relational database.

SSL (secure sockets layer). A protocol from Netscape that provides secure transactions over the Web. SSL provides authentication as well as encryption and is expected to be widely used for Internet transmission.

STP (shielded twisted pair). See *twisted pair.*

sysop (SYStem OPerator). Pronounced "siss-op". A person who runs an online communications system or bulletin board. The sysop may also act as a mediator for system conferences.

T1. A 1.544Mbps T-carrier channel that can handle twenty-four voice or data channels at 64kbps. The standard T1 frame is 193 bits long, holding twenty-four 8-bit voice samples and one synchronization bit. Eight thousand frames are transmitted per second.

T3. A 44.736Mbps T-carrier channel that can handle 672 voice or data channels at 64kbps. T3 requires fiber optic cable.

TCP/IP (Transmission Control Protocol/Internet Protocol).   A communications protocol developed under contract from the U.S. Department of Defense to network dissimilar systems. It is a de facto UNIX standard, but is now supported on almost all platforms. TCP/IP is the protocol of the Internet.

telecommuting.   Working at home and communicating with the office by electronic means.

Telnet.   A terminal emulation protocol commonly used on the Internet. It allows a user to log onto and run a program from a remote terminal or computer. Telnet was originally developed for ARPANET and is part of the TCP/IP communications protocol.

Token Ring.   A LAN developed by IBM. It uses a token ring access method and connects up to 255 nodes in a star topology at 4 or 16 Mbps. All stations connect to a central wiring hub called the MAU (multi-station access unit) using a twisted wire cable.

trading partner.   A company that exchanges business transactions with other companies using EDI.

translation software.   A software program used to convert data from one format to another, as in converting data from EDI format to an internal company format.

twisted pair.   A thin-diameter wire (22 to 26 gauge) commonly used for telephone wiring. The wires are twisted around each other to minimize interference from other twisted pairs in the cable. Twisted pairs have less bandwidth than coaxial cable or optical fiber. The two major types are unshielded twisted pair (UTP) and shielded twisted pair (STP). UTP is popular because it is very pliable and doesn't take up as much room in ductwork as does shielded twisted pair and other cables.

URL (uniform resource locator).   The Internet addressing scheme that defines the route to a file or program. For example, a home page on the Web is accessed via its URL. URLs are used as the initial address to a resource, and they are embedded within Web (HTML) documents to provide a hypertext link to another document, local or remote.

UTP (unshielded twisted pair).   See *twisted pair.*

VAN (value-added network).   A communications network that provides services beyond normal transmission, such as automatic error detection and correction, protocol conversion and message storing and forwarding.

VAR (value added reseller).   An organization that adds value to a system and resells it. For example, it could purchase a CPU (central processing unit) and peripherals from different vendors, graphics software from another, and package it all together as a specialized workflow system. Although VARs typically repackage products, they might also include programs they have developed themselves.

version control.   The management of source code, bitmaps, documents, and related files in a large software project. Version-control software provides a database that is used to keep track of the revisions made to a program or document.

video conferencing.   A video communications session among several people that are geographically separated. This form of conferencing started with room systems where groups of people meet in a room with a wide-angle camera and large monitors and conference with other groups at remote locations.

virus. Software used to infect a computer. After the virus code is written, it is buried within an existing program. Once that program is executed, the virus code is activated and attaches copies of itself to other programs in the system. Infected programs copy the virus to other programs.

VisiCalc. The first electronic spreadsheet. It was introduced in 1978 for the Apple II. Conceived by Dan Bricklin, a Harvard student, and programmed by a friend, Bob Frankston, it became a major success. It launched an industry and was almost entirely responsible for the Apple II being used in business. Thousands of $3,000 Apples were bought to run the $150 VisiCalc.

Visual Basic. A version of the BASIC programming language from Microsoft specialized for developing Windows applications. User interfaces are developed by dragging objects from the Visual Basic Toolbox onto the application form.

VRML (virtual reality modeling language). The specification for a 3-D graphics language for the Web. After downloading a VRML page, its contents can be viewed, rotated, and manipulated, and simulated rooms can be "walked into". The VRML viewer is launched from within the Web browser.

WAN (wide area network). A communications network that covers a wide geographic area, such as a state or country. A LAN is contained within a building or complex, and a MAN generally covers a city or suburb.

watermark. See *digital watermark.*

WAV. A Windows sound file, which uses the ".WAV" extension.

Web page. A page in a World Wide Web document.

Web site. A server that contains Web pages and other files, and that is online on the Internet twenty-four hours a day.

wireless technologies. Based on radio transmission via the airwaves. Various communications techniques are used to provide wireless transmission, including infrared line of sight, cellular, microwave, and satellite.

workflow. The automatic routing of documents to the users responsible for working on them. Workflow is concerned with providing the information required to support each step of the business cycle. The documents may be physically moved over the network or maintained in a single database, with the appropriate users given access to the data at the required times. Triggers can be implemented in the system to alert managers when operations are overdue.

World Wide Web. An Internet function that links documents locally and remotely. The Web document is called a Web page, and links in the page let users jump from page to page (hypertext) whether the pages are stored on the same server or on servers around the world. The pages are accessed and read via a Web browser such as Netscape Navigator or Microsoft Internet Explorer.

WORM (write once read many).   An optical disk that can be recorded only once.

X12.   An ANSI standard protocol for EDI.

year 2000 problem.   The year 2000 presents a problem for many legacy systems whose databases were designed with two-byte year fields. Years ago, saving two bytes in a record meant a lot more than it does today. A "00" in the year field is assumed to mean the year 1900, and financial calculations that deal with aging will be incorrect. You may see the abbreviations "yak" or "Y2k," which are shorthand for "year 2000".

AICPA Information Technology Membership Section
Information Technology for CPAs by CPAs

Keeping up with information technology can be a full-time job. The AICPA Information Technology Membership Section makes it easy for you to stay current on the latest technology and its uses, offering unbiased professional advice written for CPAs by CPAs that can help you make and save money. Membership in the Section is open to all AICPA members and qualifying non-CPAs at all levels of technology expertise. Just take a look at what the Information Technology Membership Section has to offer . . .

Publications

The AICPA Information Technology Membership Section publishes these documents to help accountants obtain an understanding of the technologies that face them today as well as those they will face in the future. In addition, a handsome binder is provided for you to keep your newsletters and alerts neatly and conveniently within reach.

> **Bimonthly Newsletter**—*InfoTech Update*. A 12-page newsletter filled with practical articles on dealing with technology.

> **Technology Alerts**—One-page alerts discussing "hot technology topics". Topics have included *What's Hot, What's Not: COMDEX 96; IIPCs and Windows CE—Worth the Wait?; The 809 Area Code. . .; The Year 2000. . .; Electronic Cookies. . .; Windows 95 Virus Reported. . .; Java. . .; SoftRAM95: Memory Enhancer or Snake Oil?; AOLGOLD Trojan Program;* and more. Alerts are issued periodically according to what is going on in the InfoTech environment.

Members of the AICPA Information Technology Section receive these publications as they are released as a benefit of their membership.

Discount Offerings

Currently in place, a discount program containing the *CPAs Internet Reference Guide* and the *Internet Bulletin for CPAs* is currently available. In addition, Section members receive a 35 percent discount on the purchase of the book *EDI Control, Management and Audit Issues* (1995, Product No. 043004, $19.50) for IT Section members. Further, section members receive discounts on subscriptions to *Franklynn Peterson's CPA Computer Report* as well as *The CPA Software News* and other relevant publications.

If you're still not sure what membership in the Information Technology Membership Section can do for you, call the AICPA and we'll be glad to discuss the Section with you! Call or fax:

> Andrew R. Gioseffi, CPA
> Information Technology Membership Section
> Phone: (212) 596-6211
> FAX: (212) 596-6025 Fax
> email: infotech@aicpa.org

The current annual fee for membership in the AICPA Information Technology Section is $100 for AICPA members and $165 for non-CPA Section associates for the period August 1 through July 31. Considering membership midyear? No problem. The AICPA prorates the dues schedule in the first partial year. Call for further details.

If you want to keep up with the technology, join the Information Technology Membership Section today! Don't miss out on another newsletter, publication, or discount program.

MEMBERSHIP APPLICATION FORM

AICPA Information Technology Membership Section

Please enroll me as a member in the AICPA Information Technology Membership Section through July 31. I understand that the $100.00 ($165.00) dues fee covers all membership benefits.

Signature: _____

Name: _____

Firm: _____

Address: _____

City: _____ State: _____ Zip: _____

Member Number: _____

Business Telephone: _____

Mail or Fax to:

Andrew R. Gioseffi, CPA
Information Technology Membership Section
American Institute of CPAs
1211 Avenue of the Americas
New York, NY 10036-8775
Fax: (212) 596-6025

Please note that the dues will be prorated, based on when you enroll.